"William Greenway shows that love for all creatures lies at the very center of our primeval narrative tradition. If this point sinks into the heart of the church, animals in the United States may get a fighting chance to have their dignity respected."

— CHARLES C. CAMOSY
author of *For Love of Animals:
Christian Ethics, Consistent Action*

"The popular view of the seven-days-of-creation story in Genesis is that it offers human beings divine license to instrumentalize and dominate other creatures of lesser value. With prophetic passion and scholarly precision, but without sentimentality or undue idealism, Greenway unravels this tragically flawed interpretation and weaves in its place a grace-drenched vision of creation as primordially, ultimately, and entirely beloved of God. . . . If contemporary heirs to the seven-days narrative could find the spiritual imagination to read their primeval history as Greenway does and the moral courage to live toward this vision, the world would have a great deal more joy and delight and decidedly less needless suffering and death."

— MATTHEW C. HALTEMAN
Calvin College
Oxford Centre for Animal Ethics

For the Love of All Creatures

The Story of Grace in Genesis

William Greenway

WILLIAM B. EERDMANS PUBLISHING COMPANY

GRAND RAPIDS, MICHIGAN / CAMBRIDGE, U.K.

Published 2015 by
Wm. B. Eerdmans Publishing Co.
2140 Oak Industrial Drive N.E., Grand Rapids, Michigan 49505 /
P.O. Box 163, Cambridge CB3 9PU U.K.

Printed in the United States of America

21 20 19 18 17 16 15   7 6 5 4 3 2 1

Library of Congress Cataloging-in-Publication Data

Greenway, William P.
For the love of all creatures: the story of grace in Genesis / William Greenway.
pages   cm
ISBN 978-0-8028-7291-3 (pbk.: alk. paper)
1. Creation — Biblical teaching.
2. Bible. Genesis, I-XI — Religious aspects — Christianity.
I. Title.

BS651.G775   2015
222′.1106 — dc23

2015009846

www.eerdmans.com

For Xander, Jessica, Sadie, Sherlock, and Kalico

Contents

Acknowledgments

I owe thanks to many people for supporting me in the long process of writing this book. First, I want to thank my colleagues and the trustees of Austin Presbyterian Theological Seminary, and the many students who traveled with and challenged me in my courses on "Nature, Theology, and Ethics," "Christian Creation Spirituality," "Theology and Science," and "An Adventure in Wilderness and Spirituality." A Course Prize from the Templeton Center for Theology and Natural Science and a Teaching and Learning grant from the Association of Theological Schools allowed me to pursue education in support of these courses, which proved pivotal for my reflections on the primeval history.

Second, I want to thank the folks at the many churches and institutions who so graciously hosted, questioned, and helped teach me how best to write this book. Particular thanks in this regard are due to Presbyterians for Earth Care, the Texas Interfaith Center for Public Policy, Texas Interfaith Power and Light, the Christian Vegetarian Association, the SoL Center (San Antonio), the Arizona Ecumenical Association (Phoenix), the Texas Campaign for the Environment, the Texas Conference of Churches, Bethany Presbyterian Church (Austin), Westminster Presbyterian Church (Nacogdoches, TX), Riviera United Methodist Church (Redondo Beach, CA), the SWIFT class of Tarrytown United Methodist Church (Austin), and University Presbyterian Church (Austin). I owe special thanks to Village Presbyterian Church (Prairie Village, Kansas) for inviting me to deliver the 2010 Meneilly Lectures (cosponsored by Pittsburgh Theological

Seminary), and to Logsdon School of Theology and Hardin Simmons University for jointly inviting me to deliver the 2009 George Knight Lectures.

Third, I want to express profound thanks to three scholars whose moral support and technical advice were absolutely essential. Prof. Patrick Miller, the Charles T. Haley Professor of Old Testament Theology Emeritus, Princeton Theological Seminary, and former president of the Society of Biblical Literature, read and commented on the whole manuscript and was a source of great assurance and advice for many years. Both personally and professionally, I am profoundly grateful to Pat, whose example as a Christian scholar I hope to emulate. Without his support, generosity, and encouragement, this book would never have been written. Prof. John ("Jack") Leax, a friend, poet, and nature essayist who penned the "Prayer for Order" (in his book *Out Walking: Reflections on Our Place in the Natural World*), with which I have been opening my classes for the last decade (usually substituting "Mother" for "Father"), also read and commented in detail on the entire manuscript, and he has provided essential encouragement to me over many years. Jack's encouragement, together with Pat's, was absolutely essential to my ability to pursue this work. Dr. Jana Reiss, a prolific author, longtime press editor, and now a prominent independent editor, commented on several chapters of the work and regularly provided encouragement and wise counsel about writing and publishing.

Finally, I would like to thank my wife, Cindy Rigby, my children, Xander and Jessica, and my mother, Sylvia Bailey Greenway, for their confidence, encouragement, provision of joy, and shared love for all creatures. I need to offer a special word of thanks to my brother-in-law, Scott Rigby, for providing crucial advice at a key juncture. Last but not least, I would like to express my thanks to the folks at the William B. Eerdmans Publishing Company, and especially to Eerdmans' longtime and celebrated editor-in-chief, Jon Pott, whose initial encouragement, early enthusiasm, and patient guidance through some dangerous waters allowed this work of personal passion to find its voice. As with Pat Miller and Jack Leax, Jon's support, vision, and quiet persistence were essential, and I deeply appreciate them. My thanks also go out to Eerdmans' Hebrew Bible expert Allen Myers for his willingness to support an interdisciplinary project, and to Reinder Van Til for his careful editing and encouragement.

Earlier versions of some portions of the material on the first Creation narrative and the contrast between dominion and domination, found in chapters 6 and 7, have appeared in two publications: "To Love as God Loves: The Spirit of Dominion," *Review and Expositor* 108, no. 1 (Winter 2011): 23-36; and "Life Sacred," in Christine Hoekenga, Ann Riggs, and Jenny Philips, eds., *God's Earth Is Sacred* (Washington, DC: National Council of Churches, 2012), and are used with permission, all rights reserved. Thanks to the editors at *Review and Expositor* and at the National Council of Churches eco-justice desk for their advice and support. Scripture quotations are from the New Revised Standard Version of the Bible, copyright 1989, National Council of the Churches of Christ in the United States of America. Used by permission. All rights reserved.

WILLIAM GREENWAY
Fall 2014

Preface

The ancient Israelites who wrote the seven-days-of-Creation and the Flood narratives of Genesis 1–11, commonly called the "primeval history," were not much like modern Westerners. The twelve tribes of Israel were far more similar to peoples such as the Haudenosaunee — also known as "The Five Nations of the Iroquois" — than to modern Westerners. The ancient Israelites were a premodern people who lived in an intimate relationship with creation and other creatures. Modern Western culture tends to alienate people from creation and creaturely existence. Because modern biblical interpretation, liberal and conservative alike, emerged and flourished in a modern Western ethos, it has been largely cut off from insights into spirituality, evil, grace, and faith that become visible when one approaches these narratives from the perspective of a people living in intimate relationship with creation. At the same time, the modern scientific questions that nowadays so provoke creationists and their secular opponents were at best marginal for the ancient Hebrews.

In the past few decades, especially as awareness of environmental challenges has grown, an increasing number of works in biblical studies have attempted to bridge this divide by attending to "green" dimensions of the Bible and theology.[1] A smaller but growing literature has focused

---

1. I depend on modern biblical scholarship for what is today hard-won but common knowledge with regard to the context and history of composition of the primeval history. In terms of the Hebrew Bible — both generally and with regard to the "greening" of biblical interpretation — I found the following studies particularly helpful in my

on biblical affirmation of love for all creatures.[2] This book joins in both of

research: Bernard Anderson, *From Creation to New Creation: Old Testament Perspec-tives* (Minneapolis: Fortress, 1994); Ann Astell and Sandor Goodhart, eds., *Sacrifice, Scripture, and Substitution: Readings in Ancient Judaism and Christianity* (Notre Dame, IN: University of Notre Dame Press, 2011); Walter Brueggemann, *Genesis*, Interpre-tation: A Bible Commentary for Teaching and Preaching, ed. Patrick Miller (Atlanta: John Knox, 1982); Ellen Davis, *Scripture, Culture, and Agriculture: An Agrarian Reading of the Bible* (Cambridge: Cambridge University Press, 2009); Terence Fretheim, *God and World in the Old Testament: A Relational Theology of Creation* (Nashville: Abingdon, 2005); Donald E. Gowan, *Genesis 1–11: From Eden to Babel* (Grand Rapids: Eerdmans, 1988); Theodore Hiebert, *The Yahwist's Landscape: Nature and Religion in Early Israel* (Oxford: Oxford University Press, 1996); Andrew Louth, ed., *Ancient Christian Com-mentary on Scripture: Old Testament, I, Genesis 1–11* (Downers Grove, IL: InterVarsity, 2001); Thomas Mann, *The Book of the Torah: The Narrative Integrity of the Pentateuch* (Atlanta: John Knox, 1988); Victor Matthews and Don Benjamin, *Old Testament Paral-lels*, 3rd rev. ed. (Mahwah, NJ: Paulist Press, 2006); Ernest Nicholson, *The Pentateuch in the Twentieth Century: The Legacy of Julius Wellhausen* (Oxford: Oxford University Press, 1998); Gerhard Von Rad, *Genesis: A Commentary*, rev. ed. (Philadelphia: Westminster, 1972); Ronald A Simkins, *Creator and Creation: Nature in the Worldview of Ancient Israel* (Peabody, MA: Hendrickson, 1994); John Walton, *Genesis 1 as Ancient Cosmology* (Wi-nona Lake, IN: Eisenbrauns, 2011); Claus Westermann, *Genesis: A Practical Commen-tary*, trans. David Green (Grand Rapids: Eerdmans, 1987); Claus Westermann, *Genesis 1–11: A Commentary*, trans. John Scullion (Minneapolis: Augsburg, 1974). I would also highlight the theological reflections of Michael Welker's *Creation and Reality*, trans. John F. Hoffmeyer (Minneapolis: Fortress, 1999). For a survey of major trends in the "greening" of Christian theology in the twentieth century, see William Greenway and Janet Parker, "Greening Theology and Ethics: Five Contemporary Approaches," *Reli-gious Studies Review* (January 2001): 3-9.

2. There is now a vast literature on "animal rights" or "creature care" or "love for all animals" that stretches across faith traditions and academic disciplines. Among volumes I have found especially helpful are: Carol Adams, *The Sexual Politics of Meat: A Feminist Vegetarian Critical Theory* (New York: Continuum, 2000); Margaret Barker, *Creation: A Biblical Vision for the Environment* (New York: T&T Press, 2010); Celia Dean-Drummond and David Clough, eds., *Creaturely Theology: On God, Humans and Other Animals* (Lon-don: SCM Press, 2009); David Horrell, Cherryl Hunt, Christopher Southgate, and Fran-cesca Stavrakopoulou, eds., *Ecological Hermeneutics: Biblical, Historical and Theological Perspectives* (London: T&T Clark, 2010); J. R. Hyland, *God's Covenant with Animals: A Biblical Basis for the Humane Treatment of All Creatures* (New York: Lantern Books, 2000); Andrew Linzey, *Animal Theology* (Chicago: University of Illinois Press, 1995); Andrew Linzey, *Animal Gospel* (Louisville: Westminster John Knox, 1998); Andrew Linzey and Dorothy Yamamoto, eds., *Animals on the Agenda: Questions about Animals for Theology and Ethics* (Chicago: University of Illinois Press, 1998); Jay B. McDaniel, *Of God and Pel-

these efforts, but it is also distinctive, for in the course of reading the primeval history from an overtly creaturely and creature-loving perspective, I have been opened to distinctive ways in which the primeval history, and particularly the Flood and seven-days-of-Creation narratives, inspire not only care for creation and love for all creatures but sophisticated understandings of the nature of faith, grace, and evil that are of vital moment for twenty-first-century spirituality.

I argue that an awakening to having been seized by love for all creatures lies at the heart of the ancient Israelite spirituality manifest in the primeval history. Anyone awakened to love for all creatures will be infinitely sensitive to the suffering that suffuses creation. Accordingly, the primeval history gives evil full due. Indeed, the ancient Israelites place the horrific Flood narrative at the very heart of the primeval history. Eyes wide open to the suffering of all creatures, the ancient Israelites testify to an awakening to gracious love so profound and all-embracing that, despite all the evil, one is ushered into the glory of a living faith that is the gift of grace.

My argument unfolds as follows. First, in the modern Western context it is difficult to speak reasonably and wisely about the primeval history, and particularly about the Creation and Flood narratives. This is the result of a widespread, confused, noisy, and often vehement rejection of the primeval history *on scientific grounds,* and also because of an equally widespread, confused, noisy, and often vehement defense of the primeval history *as accurate science.* There is no doubt that there are many forms of wisdom to be found in the primeval history (I am certainly not claiming to be offering the only valid interpretation); but just as surely, there are

---

icans: A Theology of Reverence for Life (Louisville: Westminster John Knox, 1989); Sallie McFague, *Super, Natural Christians: How We Should Love Nature* (Minneapolis: Fortress, 1997); Charles Pinches and Jay McDaniel, eds., *Good News for Animals? Christian Approaches to Animal Well-Being* (Maryknoll, NY: Orbis Books, 1993); Matthew Scully, *Dominion: The Power of Man, the Suffering of Animals, and the Call to Mercy* (New York: St. Martin Griffin, 2002); Manish Vyas, ed., *Issues in Ethics and Animal Rights* (Delhi: Regency Publications, 2011); Paul Waldau and Kimberley Patton, eds., *A Community of Subjects: Animals in Religion, Science, and Ethics* (New York: Columbia University Press, 2006); and Stephen H. Webb, *On God and Dogs: A Christian Theology of Compassion for Animals* (Oxford: Oxford University Press, 1998). For a brief recent history of mainstream consideration of the topic, see my entry entitled "Animals," in Joel Green, ed., *Dictionary of Scripture and Ethics* (Grand Rapids: Baker Academic, 2011), pp. 69-71.

interpretations that are confused (if well meaning). Rejecting the Creation narratives as bad science or affirming them as scientifically true gets us mixed up in a confused interpretation. It is the task of my first chapter, "Genesis 1–11: A Spiritual Classic," to clarify the character of the primeval history's authority and wisdom.

In chapter 2, "Enuma Elish: The Ancient Near Eastern Counterpoint," I review the Babylonian creation narrative that was, when the primeval history reached its extant form, the major alternative creation narrative for the ancient Israelites. Distinctive elements of the primeval history, when we read them in tandem with the Enuma Elish, stand out in clear relief. In later chapters I criticize the Enuma Elish, though it is insightful in many ways, not so much for being wrong as for lacking vital depth of discernment in comparison to the primeval history of Genesis.

In chapter 3, "*The Leviathan:* The Modern Western Counterpoint," I closely review essential elements of Thomas Hobbes's *Leviathan* in order to make clear key dimensions of the major alternative modern Western creation narrative. This narrative is loosely called "Darwinism." Note that I will be criticizing Darwinism insofar as it functions *as a creation narrative* (some people say "cosmogony"), though I accept evolution as a biological theory. In later chapters I criticize Hobbes's *Leviathan*, though it is insightful in many ways, not so much for being wrong as for lacking vital depth of discernment when compared to both the Enuma Elish and the primeval history of Genesis.

In the balance of the book, I unfold distinctive meanings manifest in the Flood and in the seven-days-of-Creation narratives when read from an overtly creaturely and creature-loving perspective. In chapter 4 ("The Genesis Flood: Shattering Violence") and chapter 5 ("Aftermath: The Birth of the God of Grace"), I read the narrative of the Flood and the rainbow covenant as the originating Creation/Fall/salvation narrative in Genesis. More precisely, I read it as the narrative that depicts the birth of the realization that love is primordial and ultimate, that love is divine, that God is love. This is not a conclusion the narrative leads one to logically infer; the dynamic is infinitely more intimate. In the direct face of all the death and suffering of the Flood, the narrative strives to awaken us so that we might find ourselves directly seized by love — and also seized by the realization that love is the primordial and ultimate reality (i.e., "alpha and omega").

Let me digress momentarily to note that I did not turn to these Jewish and Christian scriptures because I knew ahead of time that they were true, but in order to see whether or not they had something true to say. It is no accident that I turned to these texts in the first place. People generally turn first to spiritual classics such as the primeval history because many generations of people over millennia have preserved the texts and affirmed them to be founts of spiritual wisdom. For analogous reasons, people typically turn first to philosophical and literary classics. There, too, no one knows ahead of time whether or not they will prove helpful, but it is prudent to consult classics first in a quest for insight.

Moreover, my argument is wholly philosophical. It does not depend on claims to biblical infallibility or the presumed truth of any particular confession or creed. I am a Christian reflecting on Hebrew and Christian Scripture, but my argument meets public criteria of reasonableness and should succeed to the degree readers are open and find the argument personally compelling, reasonable, and subject to historically deep and culturally wide intersubjective confirmation. My argument is not disqualified from public claims to reasonableness simply because the texts I focus on are considered scriptural by two major world religions. That would be a bizarre, unjustified contention. Indeed, my argument may help explain why these texts ever attained and deserve status as transcending classics.

Parallel reasoning pertains to the classic texts and teachings of all the world's great wisdom traditions. I do not explore other religious traditions here, but I suspect and hope that the essentially Christian spirituality (and, I believe, the essentially Jewish spirituality) unfolded here would also find significant cross-cultural confirmation in Islamic, Hindu, and Buddhist texts and teachings, among many others.

I make one final preliminary note: because in Genesis 1–11 we find ourselves seized by the primordial reality of love directly in the face of massive suffering and injustice, modernity's so-called problem of evil is definitively displaced. The ancient Israelites did not theorize the existence of a perfectly good God who created a peaceable world only then to bump up against the problem of evil. The ancient Israelites, intimately acquainted with political violence, enslavement, and the daily mortal threat of illness, vipers, and predators, are utterly realistic from the beginning. Their primeval history neither denies the enduring reality of evil nor posits any heavenly life after death (though for reasons consistent with the spirituality of the primeval history, hope in a "new heaven and new earth" does eventually arise). Precisely as they stand, eyes wide open to all the horrors of the Flood — and by extension to all the other suffering that suffuses creation, they are seized by the realization that love is divine, that God is love, that God, despite the enduring evil, is the primordial and ultimate reality.

In chapter 6 ("The Seven Days of Creation"), chapter 7 ("Dominion versus Domination: Living Life and Living Death"), and chapter 8 ("A Knowing Idealism: The Decisive Asymmetry"), I argue that the seven-days-of-Creation narrative's knowingly idealistic portrayal of a perfectly perfect world is designed to awaken us to the reality and fullness of a primordial and ultimate love that prevails even in the face of injustice and suffering. I affirm both *Leviathan* and the Enuma Elish as insightful, but I argue that both fall short insofar as they do not reflect an awakening to the transcending reality of love.

The primeval history sees further than do the Enuma Elish and *Leviathan*, for it realizes that awakening to having been seized by love for every creature of every kind — the love in which we live and move and have our being — is awakening to life lived in the light of having been seized by grace. In other words, awakening to having been seized in and by love *is* awakening to the life of faith. Thus do I conclude in chapter 9, "The Primeval History: Spiritually Accurate, Realistic, and Profound," that the primeval history — and especially the Flood and seven-days-of-Creation narratives, eyes wide open to all the suffering and injustice that suffuse creation — strives to awaken us to love for all creatures so profound and all-embracing that, despite all the evil, we are ushered into the glory of a living faith that is the gift of grace.

CHAPTER ONE

Genesis 1–11

....

A Spiritual Classic

It should seem natural and wise, when seeking spiritual wisdom, to turn to classic spiritual writings. Unfortunately, "spiritual classic" and "spiritual wisdom" are not what most turn-of-the-millennium Westerners think of when they refer to the Genesis Flood and seven-days-of-Creation narratives. There are four major reasons a turn to these narratives may be surprising, especially in light of my claim to be committed to wholly reasonable investigation. First, because in the modern West the invocation of Scripture so often amounts to nothing more than an indefensible appeal to authority, and any such appeal would immediately vitiate any claim my argument may have to reasonableness.

Second, because the seven-days-of-Creation narrative is notorious for its "subdue the earth" and "have dominion" proclamations, which have been widely and justifiably blamed for promoting human exploitation of the earth and of nonhuman creatures.

Third, because the Flood narrative is on its face highly offensive, seemingly painting the picture of a reactionary god who viciously destroys almost all families of all kinds on the earth in a wildly disproportionate and wholly ungracious (to say the least) reaction to sin.

Fourth, because these narratives are Exhibit A in strident debates over creation science and the "flood geology" of young-earth creationists, and since the scientific approach to Scripture presumed by creation science is indefensible, it might seem that I should, by default, dismiss the Flood and Creation accounts as nothing more than the hopelessly outdated and obviously incorrect science of a primitive people.

All four reasons for surprise concerning a turn to the Flood and seven-days-of-Creation accounts are understandable. They involve reactions to influential modern readings of the Flood and seven-days-of-Creation narratives. However, these readings are distorted. The distortions are largely the result of modern Western tendencies to philosophical materialism (defined below) and anthropocentrism. Unfortunately, the distorted interpretations of these narratives, which are highly influential across the globe, both marginalize their stunning spiritual insight and elide all non-human creatures from our moral vision, facilitating their abuse in modern Western culture. I will argue that this moral elision and ethical abuse violates the heart of the testimony of these very narratives.

I will address issues of "subdue," "have dominion," and the violence of the Flood narrative in due course. But through the balance of this chapter I will work to address the issues of biblical authority and of the relationship of Scripture and science. First, I defend my appeal to these passages of Scripture as revelatory and distinguish my appeal from illegitimate appeals to authority. Second, I explain why many read the Flood and seven-days-of-Creation narratives as scientific accounts, and explain how these narratives themselves clearly tell us that they are not scientific. Third, I consider — as a contrasting case — a passage of Hebrew Scripture that *is* primarily scientific. Fourth, I clarify the general context within which the Flood and seven-days-of-Creation narratives reached their mature form, and thereby I clarify the signal spiritual questions these narratives originally addressed. I hope that, by the close of this brief analysis, I can disarm illegitimate appeals to authority, disarm the confusion of reading the Flood and Creation narratives as if they are primitive stabs at science, and characterize a legitimate way of hearing these spiritually profound narratives.

1. Legitimate Turn to Scripture

The Flood and seven-days-of-Creation narratives are at the heart of the so-called "primeval history" that stands at the very beginning of the Jewish and Christian scriptures in chapters one through eleven of the book of Genesis. Centuries before the time of Jesus, the primeval history had already earned its authoritative place at the very beginning of the ancient Israelites' most revered writings. The primeval history, then, is an ancient narrative that had tremendous influence on Judaism and Christianity.

While it is an ancient narrative, the primeval history is itself the product of a rich, centuries-long history of redaction ("redaction" stands for the editing and reediting of oral and written texts by diverse authors and/or communities of religious leaders). For instance, the primeval history reached its present form in Israel's late exilic or early postexilic period, around 500 BCE, whereas the earliest written versions of Ancient Near Eastern flood narratives are dated to around 1700 BCE.[1] As will become clear, the primeval history makes no attempt to hide the fact that it integrates multiple strands of extant traditions, the roots of which stretch to the earliest reaches of Israelite spirituality.

By the time the primeval history was redacted into the form we now find in Genesis, the centuries-old oral and textual traditions that the redactors were combining and revising into the Genesis version had already garnered considerable religious and political authority within the community. Therefore, as a matter of sincere respect and perhaps also serious political expedience, those authoritative narratives had to be recontextualized with considerable care. Therefore, while the primeval history is an ancient and influential narrative, it is itself a relatively late writing; and though it retains intact strands of more ancient narratives, taken as a whole in its present form, it represents one of the more mature strands of ancient Israelite spirituality in the Hebrew scriptures of Judaism and Christianity.

It is reasonable to expect narratives with such a rich and fluid history of composition and maturation, narratives that over the centuries became established and were refined as spiritual classics, to be founts of spiritual wisdom. Insofar as similar histories of composition hold for narratives among all the world's classic wisdom traditions, this conclusion holds for the spiritual classics of all the world's religions. One certainly cannot conclude from this that spiritual classics are inerrant or infallible. Nor is any revelation or truth contained *in* such narratives, such that it could be

---

1. Stephanie Dalley, trans. and ed., *Myths from Mesopotamia: Creation, the Flood, Gilgamesh and Others* (Oxford: Oxford University Press, 1989), p. 234.

extracted from them by the application of the right method. That is, I do not accept the pseudoscientific idea that revelation is some sort of propositional deposit that can be objectively mined out of a text if one applies the right methodological tools. Moreover, I never wish to be heard saying anything as self-alienating and spiritually stultifying as "Do or think this because the Bible says so."

I will not be seeking any set of objective, propositional meanings in these texts. I will not be asking, "What did the authors mean?" I will be engaged in spiritual philosophy, in a reasonable awakening to spiritual truths that I do not demonstrate, prove, construct, or in any other way originate, in a reasonable awakening to spiritual truths by which I hope we find ourselves seized. I will be asking: What spiritual awakening inspired these authors to write these texts? Or, what is the character of the spirituality to which these texts testify? In other words, what I will be saying is this: Here is classic spiritual testimony, testimony that matured over the course of centuries, testimony that stood the test of time, testimony that the Jewish and Christian traditions came to affirm as most wise and true. Do you hear it? Are you moved and convicted? More specifically, are you seized by love for every creature? These are the key questions, for the Flood and seven-days-of-Creation narratives become legitimate, truth-bearing testimony only insofar as they awaken us spiritually.

The truth-bearing potential of spiritual narratives is ever and only contemporaneous with and realized in the event of a reader's awakening. The authority of the narratives cannot be — and never should be — dogmatically asserted. And the authority of the narrative is not immanent within the text. It obtains only in the reader's having been awakened to some transcending truth. Reasonable affirmation comes in the face of this wholly subjective dynamic insofar as the awakening is logically consistent and subject to broad intersubjective confirmation: the broader and more diverse the confirmation, the greater the degree of confirmation.

In any case, I turn to these narratives precisely because for multitudes of people across generations and cultures, and for me personally, in a fashion consistent with classic Jewish and Christian spirituality, they have indeed proven to be revelatory guides in the struggle to stand faithfully, and even joyfully, eyes wide open to the otherwise overwhelming injustice and suffering that suffuses reality. In particular, I will argue that the Flood and seven-days-of-Creation narratives testify profoundly to the reality and implications of our having been seized by love for every creature.

In summary, my argument will not depend on convincing readers to affirm a proposition; nor will it be confirmed objectively in accord with my explanation of the argument's consistency with classic spiritual affirmations. The truth of the argument will obtain only insofar as it is logically consistent, coheres with historically deep and culturally diverse affirmation, and, most immediately, insofar as all readers find that it resonates with them and truly expresses and perhaps even helps them to more accurately understand and interpret within history the reality and implications of their own having been seized by love for every creature.

I am by nurture, profession, and conviction a Christian, so it is no accident that I turn to the Flood and seven-days-of-Creation narratives in Genesis. Nonetheless, it is not primarily or ultimately my Christian identity that dictates my turning to these texts; rather, it is the fact that I have indeed found them to be revelatory. Let me emphasize in this regard that insofar as we are dealing with divine reality, which is always interpreted within some culturally specific context but which is not primordially or ultimately culturally contingent, I would expect those from other faith traditions to find parallel revelatory resources among their own spiritual classics. But, quite naturally, it has been in contemplation of spiritual classics from my own tradition that I have found myself convicted and my understanding enhanced.

I have been awakened by the Flood and seven-days-of-Creation narratives. I have found that they testify to an overwhelming, humbling awe at the fragility and preciousness of each life. They gesture beyond all the distractions and superficialities of daily existence. They look at the harshest realities of existence. They bluntly name human selfishness, spite, and hatefulness. They stare, unblinking, at the suffering and injustice suffusing reality. And yet they still testify to and inspire wonder, love, and hope. So I turn to them for spiritual wisdom. This is a wholly reasonable turn to Scripture (and allow me to reiterate that I would expect those from other traditions to develop analogous and complementary reflections based on turns to their own scriptures and practices).[2]

---

2. I should note that most modern scholars of religion have consistently rejected

2. Not Science

For a powerful current of modern Western thought, real truths are thought to be ultimately the hard empirical truths of the physical sciences. For instance, at the outset of a book on consciousness, renowned philosopher Daniel Dennett lays out what is variously called the materialist, naturalist, physicalist, or scientistic (as opposed to "scientific") premise that anchors this powerful current of modern Western thought:

> *materialism:* there is only one sort of stuff, namely *matter* — the physical stuff of physics, chemistry, and physiology — and the mind is somehow nothing but a physical phenomenon. In short, the mind is the brain. According to the materialists, we can (in principle!) account for every mental phenomenon using the same physical principles, laws, and raw materials that suffice to explain radioactivity, continental drift, photosynthesis, reproduction, nutrition, and growth. It is one of the main burdens of this book to explain consciousness without ever giving in to the siren song of dualism.[3]

The cultural power of this position is visible in the informal consensus in modern Western society that when it comes to real truth about existence, those closest to ultimate truth are physicists; then, at the next remove, come the chemists and the biologists; then down through the more empirical social scientists, and then on to those who study archaeology, history, religions as wholly sociocultural and psychological phenomena; finally, one moves to the region where one has left the realm of truth entirely and entered the subjective sphere of aesthetics. There is no space at all on this continuum for theology or philosophy (i.e., "love of wisdom") in the classical sense — that is, as disciplines that reflect on spiritual realities.

Because of the power of this modern Western materialist bias, there is a tendency in modern Western culture to suppose that the most serious texts, those that make the most fundamental and ultimate truth claims,

---

materialist readings and have generated an array of significant and highly learned readings of these texts. Though most of those readings remain hobbled by the hyper-anthropocentrism of modernity, many are nevertheless profoundly insightful.

3. Dennett, *Consciousness Explained* (New York: Back Bay Books, 1991), p. 33.

must be scientific texts. And thus there is also a tendency in modern Western culture to think that if a text is making fundamental truth claims, and if one is to read it in the most serious way, then one will read it as a scientific text. So it is not surprising that Westerners generally — and especially those highly trained in the natural sciences in Western universities — believe that if they are to read the Flood and Creation narratives in Genesis seriously, and if they are to believe that those narratives make real and fundamental truth claims, then they must read them just as they read scientific texts.

It is no accident, then, that almost all leading creationists have earned doctorates in the hard sciences, mathematics, or logic from major Western research universities. These folks are wrong about creationism, but they are not lacking in intelligence or scientific training. For instance, Henry Morris, the father of modern creationism and Flood geology, earned a PhD in hydrology from the University of Minnesota, was an editorial board member of the *Journal of Engineering Education*, wrote a widely adopted secular textbook, *Applied Hydraulics in Engineering*, and was chair of the civil engineering department at Virginia Polytechnic University from 1957 to 1969.[4] Similarly, Duane Gish, Morris's "bulldog," has a PhD in biochemistry from the University of California, Berkeley, has been an assistant professor at the medical college of Cornell University, and has been a researcher on proteins and polypeptides for the Upjohn Company. (Further examples could easily be multiplied.)

Leading scientific critics of creationism suffer from the same genre confusion, for, like the creationists, they think that the Flood and Creation accounts in Genesis can lay claim to being truth-telling only insofar as they can be read as scientific texts. For instance, Niles Eldredge, curator in the department of invertebrates at the American Museum of Natural History, contends that the "cosmology of Genesis represents the best thinking available at the time. It does not have to be true to be utterly fascinating." Eldredge, striving to be generous, continues: "It is no insult to the intelligence of the ancients that human knowledge has increased."[5]

4. Ronald Numbers, *The Creationists* (Berkeley: University of California Press, 1992), p. 212. Henry Morris co-authored his textbook *Applied Hydraulics in Engineering* (2nd edition, Ronald Press Co., 1963) with James Wiggert.

5. Niles Eldredge, *Dominion* (Berkeley: University of California Press, 1995), p. 100.

Nonetheless, Eldredge is unambiguous about how we should now regard the creation narratives vis-à-vis not only science but any wisdom they may contain: "We need to get beyond such myths — accurate as they were 10,000 years ago as an assessment of the human condition."[6]

In short, creationists and their opponents in the battles over creation science all agree on one key point: the Creation and Flood accounts in Genesis make serious truth claims only insofar as they make scientific truth claims. This means that, while the creationists are right to be suspicious of materialism, they confusedly adopt a materialist understanding about truth and the genre of the Creation and Flood accounts. As these examples illustrate, modern Western belief about the ultimate character of reality and truth has given potent impetus to genre confusion among theists and atheists alike.

Why shouldn't we consider the Genesis Flood and Creation narratives to be ancient stabs at science? Why shouldn't we think that the Genesis narratives are more like Galileo than Shakespeare? Isn't it obvious that the ancient Israelites would have read the Genesis Creation and Flood narratives as science? Actually, as biblical scholars have long realized, the primeval narrative itself clearly says "no." I shall leave aside myriad significant considerations and focus on just one reason for drawing this conclusion: the scientific/historical incompatibility of the two creation narratives at the beginning of Genesis.

It is clear that there are two creation narratives at the beginning of Genesis. The first narrative is the well-known seven-days-of-Creation narrative with which Genesis opens (Gen. 1:1–2:3). The second, which begins where the first leaves off, is the equally well-known Adam-and-Eve narrative. There are many distinctions between the two narratives. One major distinction between the two — and this is even more obvious in the original Hebrew — is that they use different names for God. In the seven-days narrative, "God" is *Elohim*. In the Adam-and-Eve narrative, "God" is *Jahweh*. This is signaled in most English translations by the use of "God" in the seven-days narrative and the use of "Lord God" in the Adam-and-Eve narrative. This does not mean that two different "Gods" are being

6. Eldredge, *Dominion*, p. xv. Eldredge pursues the same line of argument in *The Triumph of Evolution and the Failure of Creationism* (New York: Henry Holt, 2000).

referred to; it does, however, indicate two different habits of usage and almost surely indicates two narrative strata.

But the two accounts do not only use distinct vocabularies; historically and scientifically they are mutually contradictory. That is not to say that they are theologically contradictory. I will note only one of many literal contradictions: the order in which things are created is different in the two narratives. In the seven-days narrative God first creates light, then dry land and seas, then vegetation, then sun and moon and stars, then fishes and birds, then all the land animals, and, last of all, a male and female human (both created at the same time in God's image).

In the Adam-and-Eve narrative the order in which things are created is very different. First God creates Adam from dust. Then God creates all the plants, including a garden containing a tree of life and a tree of the knowledge of good and evil (once trees "of the knowledge of good and evil" start sprouting up, you can be pretty certain that you are not reading a science text on flora and fauna). Then God creates all the animals and birds. And then, after all the plants and other animals have been created, God creates the woman. This sequence of creation (i.e., male, then vegetation, then animals, then female) is obviously incompatible with the sequence in the seven-days narrative (i.e., vegetation, all animals, then male and female at the same time).

As even this cursory analysis makes visible, in a historical/scientific sense these are two mutually incompatible accounts of creation. There are basically three conclusions one might draw. First, one might conclude that the people who put these accounts together were trying to write a historically/scientifically accurate account, but they were too dull-witted to notice glaring inconsistencies. Second, one might say that, for reasons that are nowhere explained or referred to, God actually created everything twice. (This should be too absurd a possibility to mention, but in a desperate attempt to affirm the historical/scientific meaning of the text, some Christians have found themselves driven to such speculation.) Third, one might conclude that the people who composed these accounts noticed the contradictions, but that scientific or historical accuracy was not a concern of theirs because the narratives testify to other kinds of truth.

The contradictions between the two Genesis Creation narratives are so obvious that it is impossible to think that those who composed the primeval history did not notice them. And the texts themselves give us no reason to suppose that they are referring to two distinct events of creation (the concern to posit distinct acts of creation comes not from any explicit pointers in the texts, but wholly in response to the desire to read these texts as scientific/historical). So the third conclusion — that the obvious historical contradictions were noticed but considered irrelevant — is by far the most reasonable. That is, the texts themselves clearly suggest that they should be read not as one reads Galileo but as one reads Shakespeare. Indeed, it will become increasingly clear as I unfold the profound claims of these texts that there is every reason to conclude that the ancient Israelites would be stunned at the superficiality of modern scientific readings of these narratives.

For example, imagine if someone were to say, scoldingly, "*The Grinch Who Stole Christmas* is clearly false! I've checked. It turns out there's absolutely no such creature as a grinch!" That is not a very clever point. Dr. Seuss stories contain many significant truth claims, but not if you are a biologist interested in animal species and behavior. Or what about this: "All the world's a stage, and all the men and women merely players." Is this true or false? It is certainly not scientific truth. If it is Galileo versus Shakespeare, and you are talking about the physical structure of the universe, then Galileo wins and Shakespeare is pretty confused. But just as Dr. Seuss is not making a scientific claim about the existence of grinches, Shakespeare is not making a scientific claim about the world being a big stage.

To evaluate Shakespeare or Seuss by scientific standards is both ludicrous and highly significant. It is ludicrous because it so astonishingly misses the point. But it is highly significant because important truth claims *are* being made. Shakespeare's "all the world's a stage, and all the men and women merely players," for instance, is a profound affirmation of nihilism and a provocation to anomie (i.e., a sense of meaningless and purposelessness) that anticipates much nineteenth- and twentieth-century existentialism. While Dr. Seuss writings probably cannot be compared to any of Shakespeare's plays or any spiritual classics, "Grinch," with its appeal to the sustaining reality of love in community, contests the nihilism and anomie portrayed in Shakespeare.

We will miss the profound challenges and potential of Dr. Seuss and Shakespeare narratives if we read them as science. Unfortunately, this is precisely what we do when we read the Genesis Creation narratives as science. We take incredibly rich and meaningful narratives and reduce them to a primitive, mechanistic account of the physical origins of creation and the physical dimensions of the Flood. Instead of exploring the narratives for more profound testimony, we strip them down, empty them of their true significance, and reduce their revelatory potential. Plus, we get ourselves some lousy science (even by ancient Israelite standards).

3. A Primarily Scientific Biblical Text

We do the Creation narratives an injustice, then, if we read them as scientific texts. There are, however, other texts in Hebrew Scripture that are primarily scientific. In such cases, one should dismiss the primitive science, for there is no reason to expect or conclude that scientific knowledge has been magically implanted in Scripture. Consider another passage from Hebrew Scripture: Leviticus 13:29-45. "Leprous" in this passage refers to any contagious skin disease or infection, including but not limited to leprosy. As you read the passage, note that rudimentary medical methodology, no doubt derived from observation and experience, is evident. Note the ancient authors' criteria, for instance, for distinguishing the characteristics of infectious versus benign sores, and their sense for the time line over the course of which an infection either will spread and give evidence of being dangerous or else will have healed and been proved benign. Note even some advice to prevent the spread of germs (basically, "when you're contagious, warn others and cover your mouth").

> When a man or women has a disease on the head or in the beard, the priest shall examine the disease. If it appears deeper than the skin and the hair in it is yellow and thin, the priest shall pronounce him unclean; it is an itch, a leprous disease of the head or the beard. If the priest examines the itching disease, and it appears no deeper than the skin and there is no black hair in it, the priest shall confine the person with the itching disease for seven days. On the seventh day the priest shall examine the itch; if the itch has not spread, and there is no yellow hair in it, and the itch appears to be no deeper than the skin, he shall shave, but the itch he shall not shave. The priest shall confine the person with the itch for

seven days more. On the seventh day the priest shall examine the itch; if the itch has not spread in the skin and it appears to be no deeper than the skin, the priest shall pronounce him clean. He shall wash his clothes and be clean. But if the itch spreads in the skin after he was pronounced clean, the priest shall examine him. If the itch has spread in the skin, the priest need not seek for the yellow hair; he is unclean. But if in his eyes the itch is checked, and black hair has grown in it, the itch is healed, he is clean; and the priest shall pronounce him clean. . . . The person who has the leprous disease shall wear torn clothes and let the hair of his head be disheveled; and he shall cover his upper lip and cry out, "Unclean, unclean." He shall remain unclean as long as he has the disease; he is unclean. He shall live alone; his dwelling shall be outside the camp. (Lev. 13:29-46, NRSV)

This text evidently reflects basic medical knowledge built on the empirical experiences of the ancient Israelites. Again, a rudimentary methodology is evident. One reads criteria for distinguishing the characteristics of sores that are diseased versus those that are benign, and a sense for the time line over the course of which a disease will either spread and give evidence of being dangerous or heal and prove benign. One also hears unclean persons instructed to cover their nose and mouth while warning others that they have an infectious disease. I would not be surprised to learn that this is all fairly sound — if primitive — medical advice. However, if any of us today were to suffer from a serious skin condition, I would urge that person to ignore this text and seek out the most advanced medical advice available — and to act according to that advice.

On the other hand, even this text has a spiritual dimension. It offers significant commentary, for instance, on those, like priests and doctors, who would minister to people. To be a priest among the ancient Israelites was to enjoy considerable status and power. But consider the position of the priest in a primitive society. This is a society without knowledge of germs, antiseptics, or antibiotics, and the priest is regularly examining people's sores in order to determine whether or not they are contagious. To be a priest, then, meant continually putting himself at considerable risk on behalf of others and his community. In this sense, the text may bring into focus considerable and still-timely wisdom concerning ideals for ministers, doctors, and those adopting roles of leadership and power within any community. More problematically, the text reflects a marginalization of those who are ill that, while perhaps understandable among a primitive people worried about infectious diseases, should nonetheless be subject to careful critique.

There are other texts that do not arrange themselves neatly on one or the other side of this spiritual-versus-scientific divide. But it is not my goal here to enter into debates about borderline cases, but to set up a contrast that makes it clear that the Creation narratives are not scientific texts. Indeed, by this time it should be fairly obvious that the Creation narratives contrast markedly with those texts, like the Leviticus 13 medical text just cited, that are primarily scientific (more on the Flood narrative presently). But if the Creation narratives are not doing science, what are they about?

4. The Primeval History in Context

The primeval history (Gen. 1–11) is made up of a series of subnarratives together with a few genealogies. The order of the various subnarratives (namely, the seven days of Creation, Adam and Eve, Eve and the Serpent, the Flood, the Tower of Babel) roughly follows a chronological narrative logic. But the extant ordering of the subnarratives does not reflect their relative ages. For instance, in Genesis the Adam and Eve narrative comes in the text after the seven-days narrative. Yet, though it comes second, the Adam and Eve narrative is older (probably centuries older) than the seven-days narrative (which most likely does not predate the extant version of the narrative by more than a century). The origins of both narratives are shrouded in the mists of oral tradition, and the written versions were almost certainly redacted (i.e., edited and reshaped). In any case, as noted above, the primeval history in Genesis reached its final written form around the end of (or just after) the Israelites' exile in Babylon (around 500 BCE). Thus the Babylonian exile (the Israelites' "exilic period") is an excellent representative context for reading the primeval history.[7]

7. For a more detailed discussion of the dating of these (what I have said here represents what is now general consensus), see the works on Genesis, Wellhausen, and Old Testament parallels listed in the Preface, note 1 above.

Before being driven into exile in Babylon, Israel had been a mighty and wealthy kingdom under her three greatest kings: Saul, David, and Solomon. In the generations after the reign of Solomon, however, the Israelites suffered from corrupt rule, civil wars, fragmentation of the nation, and military defeats. Eventually, the surviving tribes of the once mighty nation suffered total defeat at the hands of the Babylonians. The Israelites were marched into exile from Israel to Babylon (near present-day Baghdad), where they lived for generations as the subjects of a people who worshiped other gods.

In the midst of their defeat and exile, some Israelites most likely came to the very reasonable conclusion that their god must not be the God of all the earth after all (for their god had evidently lost to the Babylonian gods). These Israelites most likely assimilated themselves quite nicely into Babylonian society. Others, however, remained faithful to the God who had led them out of Egypt and made them a great nation under David. These Israelites interpreted the exile as a time of judgment. They looked to learn from their experience of exile. They tried to become a more faithful people. And they dreamed of a return to their ancestral home. It is the perspective and, more importantly, the nascent theology of these Israelites, who refused to assimilate and who interpreted the exile as an awful period of alienation from their land and their Temple, which is represented and affirmed in the primeval history of Genesis. The primeval history was originally striving to address the urgent concerns and pressing questions of these Israelites.

In the midst of their defeat and captivity, primordial moral and spiritual questions came to the fore. What of all the wondrous beauty and joy? What of all the unspeakable suffering and death? Why all the oppression and injustice? Why the horrible evils? For what might we hope? How should we live? Who, how, and what shall we love? Such spiritual questions are *the* questions of life. They are the most profound and troubling questions haunting human hearts and minds. They are the questions that animate our greatest poets, painters, and saints. And they are the fundamental questions animating the Creation and Flood narratives.

Science brilliantly facilitates full appreciation of the physical complexity of the world. And science now provides previously undreamt-of power for prediction of and control within the world. But if we have no orientation to the spiritual questions of life, then all of the technical knowledge and technology in the world is at best empty and useless and at worst destructive and evil. Not even the most advanced technical understanding about how the world works can tell us how the world should work, or tell us how we should react to the world, or whether or not there is anyone or any way beyond the systems of this world in which we might hope. On the other hand, the more clarity and resolve we have with regard to what is loving, good, and just, the more scientific knowledge and technology can become resources for great good and blessing.

In short, by definition, science cannot speak to spiritual questions, let alone pass judgment on the reality or character of the divine. The primeval history of Genesis, by contrast, is speaking precisely to spiritual questions, and is confessing the Israelites' faith about the character and reality of the divine. Attention to context leads us again to the conclusion that the Flood and seven-days-of-Creation narratives address not scientific but spiritual questions, questions of suffering and joy, of good and evil, justice and injustice, life and death, and of hope. To the degree that these ancient narratives advance scientific claims, it is foolish to heed them. At the same time, to the degree that these or any of humanity's other spiritual classics address spiritual questions, it is foolish to dismiss them out of hand.

The ancient Israelites were no fools. They understood that knowing how the world works is critical to survival. And, it is important to recall, they understood how the world really works well enough to survive in wilderness conditions that would soon kill most modern Westerners. But they also realized that all such knowledge is empty if you do not have a clue about the spiritual dimensions of life.[8]

Imagine this. You're an oncologist. A dear friend has just found that the bothersome pain in her husband's back is actually cancer. It has already spread. There is no hope. She is weeping bitterly, and she cries out to you,

---

8. Given the current significance of the creation/evolution controversies, let me state explicitly that I have considerable sympathy for creationists when it comes to rebutting a widespread and smug dismissal of the Flood and Creation narratives as *nothing but* primitive science, for the spiritual claims of these narratives remain vital in our day. Nonetheless, insofar as these texts do presume ancient scientific understandings of the workings of the cosmos, they are unquestionably primitive, and their scientific understanding should be dismissed.

"Why? Why?" Do you do your best to explain scientifically how cancer originates, develops, and spreads? No. That would be a devastating misunderstanding of her question. Her cry of "Why? Why?" is a spiritual cry, not a scientific question.

In the same way, when the Israelites cried out "Why? Why?" amid their captivity and exile, they were not asking a scientific question. And the spiritual leaders who redacted the Flood and Creation narratives were not foolish enough to offer up a scientific reply. Naturally the narratives presumed contemporary scientific understanding — we should expect nothing else — but the scientific precision was not the concern. The anguished question is spiritual, and the testimony of the Flood and Creation narratives is likewise spiritual. So the tendency to read spiritual classics as if they are scientific misunderstands and diminishes them terribly.

Once cleansed of materialist tendencies and misunderstandings, and once freed from spiritually empty appeals to authority, not only Jews and Christians but everyone who is spiritually driven and curious can and should approach spiritual classics such as the flood and creation narratives in Genesis not only with due critical suspicion, but with openness and even hopeful expectation. Of course, with regard to the Flood and seven-days-of-Creation narratives in particular, we also need to take special care to rid ourselves of the anthropocentrism that has plagued readings of these texts for two millennia, and which in the modern West has been amplified to devastating levels.

In order for those of us who are influenced by modern Western thought to read the Flood and seven-days-of-Creation narratives in Genesis with adequate sensitivity to the context and competing background ideas that both the ancient Hebrews and we bring into play, it is important that we have some explicit awareness of two highly influential and competing "creation" narratives. First is the Enuma Elish, the creation narrative of the Babylonians, who defeated the ancient Israelites and in whose land the Israelites were exiled for generations. (The Enuma Elish was *the* competing creation narrative for the ancient Israelites who authored/redacted our received version of the Creation and Flood narratives in Genesis.)

Second, it is important that we have some familiarity with the seventeenth-century philosopher Thomas Hobbes's seminal work *Levia-*

than, which, in combination with evolutionary theory, offers an explicit philosophical articulation of what was to become the modern West's materialist creation narrative. *Leviathan* itself will be unfamiliar to most modern Westerners; however, as will become clear, the book's main themes are entirely familiar, for Hobbes brilliantly anticipates and clearly articulates the spiritual, moral, and political implications of philosophical materialism. And insofar as Hobbesian/Darwinian-style materialism constitutes the predominant modern Western understanding of the ultimate character of reality, *Leviathan* (or, at any rate, the positions it first articulated) represents *the* competing creation narrative in modern Western thought. So I now turn to "Enuma Elish: The Ancient Near Eastern Counterpoint" (chapter 2) and "*Leviathan:* The Modern Western Counterpoint" (chapter 3).

CHAPTER TWO

Enuma Elish

....

The Ancient Near Eastern Counterpoint

1. The Enuma Elish

Every community of people (and each person within it) has some creation narrative, some notion of the primordial and ultimate character of reality, some notion of whence everything has come and whither everything is headed. Creation narratives subtly supply the background framework within which one interprets all of life, so they profoundly shape spiritual understanding and social and political life. When the primeval history, including the seven-days-of-Creation narrative, reached its final form, the ancient Israelites were emerging from generations of exile in Babylon. For those Israelites, the Epic of Creation of the Babylonians, commonly called the Enuma Elish, was the major competing creation narrative.

We know little about the origins of the Enuma Elish. Like the Creation narratives in Genesis, it may well be the product of a long oral history. At any rate, insofar as it became recognized and for centuries endured as a central spiritual text of the Babylonian empire, the Enuma Elish reflects the collective wisdom of a people, a wisdom that proved out and was almost certainly refined through periods of struggle and joy, of flourishing and suffering. Not surprisingly, the message of the Enuma Elish is realistic, reasonable and, in its subtle yet potent resistance to tyranny, cunning and relatively good (even if, particularly with regard to its sexist dynamics, it is certainly far from ideal).[1]

1. I would be more worried about sexist aspects of the Enuma Elish if I were going

18

The date of composition of the Enuma Elish is not certain, though it was composed at some point between 2000 and 1000 BCE. The epic begins with the existence of two primordial gods, Apsu (Fresh Water) and Tiamat (Sea), from whom generation upon generation of other gods have been born. It may not be coincidental that regions where rivers (i.e., fresh waters) run out into the seas are among the most biologically fertile regions on earth, and that the Enuma Elish suggests that ultimately everything that exists flows from the commingling of Apsu and Tiamat.

Over time, generation after generation of gods are born, and diverse societies of gods come into being. At one point a group of younger gods becomes raucous and disturbs the lives and peaceful rest of both Fresh Water and Sea. This is not a minor affront. The value of rest and peace is paramount in multiple ancient epics (including the seven-days-of-Creation narrative, which dedicates the entire seventh day to rest). In the face of the raucous young gods, Tiamat is indulgent; however, Apsu eventually becomes angry and goes to Tiamat with a plan to drive away the younger gods, saying, "Their ways have become grievous to me. By day I cannot rest, by night I cannot sleep. I shall abolish their ways and disperse them!"[2]

Tiamat becomes angry about Apsu's plan and urges him to be patient. Apsu, however, continues to plot "evil" for "the gods his sons." One of those gods, Ea, a "superior" god, "wise and capable," discovers Apsu's plot. Ea casts a spell on Apsu and slays him. Then, out of the "pure interior" of the slain Apsu, Ea creates a god who is vastly superior to all the other gods, Marduk: "Four were his eyes, four were his ears; When his lips moved, fire blazed forth. . . . Highest among the gods, his form was outstanding" (p. 236).

Marduk is given the four winds to play with, and with them he stirs up Sea (Tiamat). As a result of Marduk's play, many gods besides Tiamat are disturbed and unable to rest. So they approach Tiamat and agitate her even further. They ask where she was when her lover, Apsu, was slain. They suggest that Marduk is disturbing her on purpose because, instead

---

to recommend it as a model. But I will be using it only as a means of comparison, not recommending it be adopted, so I will only note the danger.

2. Stephanie Dalley, trans. and ed., *Myths from Mesopotamia: Creation, the Flood, Gilgamesh and Others* (Oxford: Oxford University Press, 1989), p. 234. Hereafter, page references to this work appear in parentheses within the text.

of aiding her lover, Apsu, she sat by quietly. And they ask why she is not taking action to help them, her sons, when Marduk, who was created by Apsu's killer, is disturbing them all (p. 236).

Tiamat is convinced by these speeches and decides to kill not only Marduk but also Ea and the whole society of gods who surround them (p. 237). Tiamat causes "Mother Huber, who fashions all things," to create fierce creatures to take into battle, "giant snakes, sharp of tooth and unsparing of fang . . . their bodies [filled] with venom instead of blood" (p. 237). Then she appoints the greatest of the gods among her sons, Qingu, to lead the battle against their enemies. In doing all of this, the epic specifies, Tiamat "did even more evil for posterity than Apsu" (p. 239).

Note that Tiamat and Apsu, the ultimate originators, are both credited primarily with having done evil. To remember this is to remember that salt water and fresh water are the source not only of life, but also of chaotic, lethal, and — as personified — murderous waters. Aside from the person-ification, this mirrors common experience even today. On the one hand, we appreciate life-giving rains that water our crops and replenish drinking water supplies, and we enjoy our rivers, lakes, and oceans as places of rec-reation, beauty, and plentiful life. On the other hand, we are all too aware of the deadly force of floods, tsunamis, and awesome ocean storms. It is not difficult to imagine, then, why ancient people might personify fresh and salt waters as capricious and chaotic givers and takers of life.

Ea learns all about Tiamat's deadly plan. He is frightened by her plan and by the terrible creatures she has created. He goes and tells his father, Anshar, about everything. Anshar, too, is fearful: "His roar to his son Ea was quite weak" (p. 241). Anshar sends Ea to Tiamat in an effort to calm her, but her response remains fierce. When Ea reports this to Anshar, he is "speechless . . . he gnashed his teeth . . . and shook his head [in despair]" (p. 242). Soon, however, Marduk comes forward, confident that he can defeat Tiamat. An assembly of the gods is called together, and Tiamat's fearsome preparations are revealed to all. Like Ea, the assembled gods are genuinely afraid. It is announced that Mar-duk has volunteered to go and face Tiamat, but there is one condition: the gods must agree that if Marduk goes and fights Tiamat and succeeds in saving their lives, then they have to make Marduk their absolute ruler (pp. 243-44). The fearful gods gladly agree to the bargain: "O Marduk, you are our champion! We hereby give you sovereignty over all of the whole universe" (pp. 248-50).

The gods rejoice at the power of Marduk and send him out to kill Tiamat (p. 250). Thus, the epic specifies, the gods, Markduk's "fathers," "set him on the path of peace and obedience" (p. 251). Marduk goes into battle with Tiamat. At first Tiamat feigns friendliness, but Marduk is not fooled. "Why," he asks Tiamat (Sea), "are you so friendly on the surface when your depths conspire to muster a battle force?" (p. 252) Throwing Tiamat's treachery in her face and accusing her of rejecting compassion, Marduk provokes Tiamat into a wild rage.

Lost in the surging forces of her rage, Tiamat makes a fatal error. Leaving Qingu and her other forces behind, she lashes out and attacks with a scream. Marduk, armed as always with the winds his father had given him, dispatches a wind to Tiamat's face. Tiamat opens her mouth to swallow it. But Marduk seizes the opportunity to force her mouth wide open and shoots an arrow into the very depths of Tiamat, slitting her heart apart and killing her (p. 252). Seeing Tiamat's defeat, Qingu and the rest of her forces are terrified and attempt to flee. But Marduk cuts off their escape, smashes their weapons, and takes them captive.

Then Marduk sends some of Tiamat's blood on the North Wind to inform his father gods of the victory. From Tiamat's corpse he creates our visible cosmos (p. 255). With one part of Tiamat he creates the night sky (p. 255); in the night sky he sets up places of special honor for select gods, the constellations of stars that designate the year and mark out the months of the year, thereby fixing human months and earthly seasons (p. 255). Out of Tiamat's liver he creates the moon, and he commands that it wax and wane on a steady monthly basis. In like fashion he creates out of Tiamat clouds, rain, springs, the Tigris and Euphrates rivers, mountains, the daytime sky, and the earth (pp. 256-57).

Marduk is celebrated and praised for his victory by all the other gods. Hearing the gods' praises and promises of fidelity, he is pleased and "makes up his mind to perform miracles" (p. 260). One miracle in particular he executes for the benefit of his subjects, the gods. He shares his plan with Ea:

Let me put blood together, and make bones too.
Let me set up primeval man: Man shall be his name.

Let me create a primeval man.
The work of the gods shall be imposed (on him),
    And so they shall be at leisure. (pp. 260-61)

Ea is pleased and makes his contribution to the "plan for the leisure of the gods," suggesting that the god who provoked Tiamat to rebellion should be made to pay the penalty for his crime — "that [the gods] may dwell in peace" (p. 261). So Qingu is seized and Ea slays him, and he "created mankind from his blood, imposed the toil of the gods (on man) and released the gods from it" (p. 261). This creation of man by Ea, the text specifies, "is impossible to describe, for Nudimmud performed it with the miracles of Marduk" (pp. 261-62). After the creation of man by Ea and/or Nudimmud using the miracles of Marduk, Marduk appoints all of the gods to their respective realms in the starry heavens and sky and on the earth. The gods, eager to please Marduk, ask him what they might do, and he commands them to build Babylon, with a high shrine in its center and dwellings for the greatest gods. Then the gods again swear their allegiance to the mighty Marduk, for "the son who avenged us shall be the highest!" (p. 264).

Marduk is likewise the defender of Man, and so Man is called to worship and respect Marduk:

Let [Marduk] act as shepherd over the black-headed people, his creation. . . . He shall take care of them, he shall look after their shrines. . . . Let him breathe on earth as freely as he always does in heaven. Let him designate the black-headed people to revere him, that mankind may be mindful of him, and name him as their god. . . . Let *nindabu*-offerings be brought to their god [and their] goddess. Let them never be forgotten! . . . Let them keep their country pre-eminent, and always build shrines. (pp. 264-65)

I should emphasize that, though I have cited from the passage concerning humans at length, only a tiny fraction of the epic is about humans. It is all, of course, written by and for humans. On the whole, the Enuma Elish is almost wholly devoted to stories of the gods. This portion of the epic is overwhelmingly devoted to the gods' praise for Marduk. That said, let me note one other set of lines in the midst of these extended praises where humans are once again mentioned: "The people whom he created, the form of life that breathes. He imposed the work of the gods [on them] so that they [the gods] might rest. Creation and abolition, forgiveness and punishment — such are at his disposal, so let them look to him" (p. 265). As is again illustrated here, on the very few occasions in which humans are mentioned, the significance of their creation for the leisure of the gods is emphasized. Notably, the narrative also specifies that Marduk is merciful because the creation of humans relieved the burden even of the "captured gods" (p. 268).

The extended passage that concludes the narrative is dedicated to singing praises to the fifty names of Marduk. In the narrative, the identities of and boundaries among the gods are sometimes imprecise and porous. For example, as we have just seen, Ea, Nudimmud, and Marduk are all given credit for creating humans. In other places — both before and after these lines — Marduk alone is praised for the act. Notably, these imprecise and porous boundaries are familiar from our own experience and naming of the forces of nature. For example, in our daily experience there is no precise boundary between fog, dew, mist, rain, sleet, and snow, just as there is no precise boundary in the especially fertile waters where rivers flow into seas (i.e., there is no precise boundary where Apsu ends and Tiamat begins).

In the extended concluding passage, the gods sing praises to Marduk in terms of fifty names, which represent fifty powers. The section is lengthy because each name is accompanied by a line, often by several lines, that explain in detail the powers associated with the various names. This gathering of names/powers under the one god, Marduk, accentuates a sense for an underlying unity among various powers and principalities. It is interesting to note in this regard that the birth of Western philosophy is today commonly marked by reference to the culminating moment of the ancient Greeks' more explicit gathering of forces under a single principle, namely, Thales's declaration that "everything is water" — that is, the origin *(arche)* of everything, the ultimate substance, is water.

Near the end of the recitation of the fifty names there is a digression that addresses humans. It specifies that no other god is to "designate the revenues of the black-headed peoples," nor are decisions about the duration of their lifetimes to be made by anyone apart from Marduk (p. 272). In other words, Marduk is the god of death and taxes! After the fifty names are celebrated, the narrative closes with a brief call for the gods always to cherish Marduk, and for father gods to instruct their sons in his ways, that the "song of Marduk" might always be remembered (pp. 273-74).

While it is tangential to my main line of inquiry, let me explicitly note the sexist character of these instructions inasmuch as no mothers or daughters are deemed worthy of mention. Of course, this sexism is consistent with the narrative's overarching portrayal of the predominant male bringing order by violently defeating the most powerful female who, though a mother of life, is also fearsome, murderous, and raging. The whole narrative, as is the case with all spiritual/religious creation narratives, is concerned with asserting a fundamental view of the ultimate character of existence. This view, of course, will legitimate some social, political, cultural, ethical, and religious institutions, and will delegitimize others. The sexism in this narrative is not innocent, then, for it creates a background framework in which sexism is woven into the very order of creation (sexist elements haunt many religious, philosophical, and scientific texts even into the twenty-first century).

2. The "What, Ultimately, Is Going On" (i.e., the Metaphysics) of the Enuma Elish

As with the seven-days and Adam-and-Eve narratives in Genesis, the Enuma Elish looks pretty unrealistic if one reads it as a scientific text in the modern sense. But again, as with the Genesis Creation narratives, to conclude that the world was created out of the body of a slain god in a literal sense would be awful science even by ancient standards. Like the ancient Israelites, the ancient Babylonians knew enough about how the real world works to survive in wilderness conditions that would quickly kill many of us. To the degree that the Enuma Elish does make scientific claims in the modern sense, one can simply ignore them, for they are tangential to the real concern of the text. As with Genesis, the central concerns of the Enuma Elish are moral and spiritual.

In the Enuma Elish there are a multitude of gods, no one of whom is necessarily supreme. Creation of an ordered realm for the gods, and

24

creation of our world and of us humans, comes about only after a real fight among the gods. The ultimate stuff out of which all godly existence is made is Apsu and Tiamat. Apsu and Tiamat are each a chaotic mix of evil and good (recall, for instance, that despite his evil deeds, Apsu is said to have had a "pure interior"). However, both are best remembered — and ultimately vanquished — for doing evil. For the Enuma Elish, then, the primordial forces of existence are morally ambiguous and tend toward evil, and only after both Apsu and Tiamat are defeated, does good establish itself as preeminent. Chaos and evil are not utterly vanquished from being. They are now held at bay thanks to the heroism, power, and cunning of Marduk.

In other words, when the ancient Babylonians considered existence, they perceived ultimate reality, the *arche* of all that is, to be good and evil mixed up in the chaos of primordial stuff. Order — and then good — finally emerge within existence through the work of (male) agents who successfully battle the forces of chaos and evil. Apsu and Tiamat signify the chaotic *arche* (i.e., metaphysical origins, ultimate character) of existence. Marduk signifies the emergence of good that is powerful enough to defeat evil, and also the continuing triumph of a good order within existence. In existence as humans know it, the chaotic, evil, and even murderous character of the Ur-gods is largely defeated. Order, justice, and even mercy can now reign.

Nonetheless, while order, justice, and even mercy now reign, chaos continually threatens and occasionally bursts forth in destructive floods, storms, drought, or disease. That is, though we live within the reign of Marduk, the ultimate stuff out of which our world is made, Tiamat and Apsu, is ever potent. Moreover, when the ancient Babylonians looked within, they concluded that the same chaotic mix of good and evil found within the gods is also within us. That is, we humans have within us the stuff of Qingu, Tiamat's co-conspirator, another god best remembered for plotting evil. So our own self-discipline and our support of solid social structures are necessary to help us bring order and good to the fore in our personal and political lives.

The narrative ends without foreboding, urging gods and people alike to continue to support the reign and to sustain the favor of Marduk, and to instruct their children to do likewise. The future, however, is fundamentally open. Chaos and evil still haunt the borders of existence. The primordial stuff out of which our whole world is made is Tiamat. And chaos and evil do not merely threaten from without; the very stuff we humans are made out of is Qingu. Chaos from without and within is held at bay only by the sustained exertion of Marduk's power, the social structures of divine and human society, and self-discipline on the part of both gods and humans. Tiamat and Apsu could at any time become resurgent. That is, as the occasional devastating flood, insurrection, or invasion would have made terribly clear to the ancient Babylonians, the forces of Tiamat and Qingu are ever lurking.

While the future is fundamentally open to chaos and evil, however, the narrative ends with optimism, celebrating Marduk's victory. Now that Tiamat is defeated, "creation and abolition, forgiveness and punishment" are at the disposal of Marduk alone. The narrative reminds us of Marduk's power with a caution and an admonition: "So let them look to him."

Note the emphasis here on Marduk's power over life, death, forgiveness, and punishment. Given Marduk's power over the likes of these, it is clearly prudent to "look to him." This is not a call to love or to worship God in the familiar spiritual sense; nor, on the other hand, is this "look to him" a blind paean to power. Marduk is held up as a god who is not only mighty but also good. He is a god who was created out of the "pure interior" of Apsu; he was from the beginning set "on the path of peace and obedience"; he created marvels for the sake of the other gods; and he is credited with "showing mercy," because when he created humans in order to free the gods from labor, he freed even the "captured gods" who rebelled with Tiamat.

Admittedly, Marduk creates humans so that we might absorb the toil that had been the burden of the gods. We are created to be, at best, servants. This means that we should understand that our comfort is not Marduk's primary concern. In particular, we humans should not expect Marduk or any other god to free us from the burdens of labor that life brings upon us, for instance, from the hard work required to get the fields to yield crops. Humans were created to bear precisely these burdens. In other words, we should be realistic about how the world works and what is necessary for us to survive in it.

On the other hand, Marduk is a god of peace and mercy. We are Marduk's subjects and his creation, and he is a god of order and goodness, so it is no surprise that he would prove to be a good master. Accordingly, the Enuma Elish calls Marduk a "shepherd" of the black-headed peoples. And it assures the people that Marduk will "take care of them" and "look after their shrines."

Not only because of his power and cunning, then, but also because Marduk is in all these ways good — and despite the fact that people were created in order to labor so that the gods might have leisure — the black-headed people are to "revere" Marduk, to "name him as their god," and to "keep their country preeminent, and always build shrines." To get an idea of the dynamics the narrative has in mind here, consider the popular reaction one would expect to a military general who has saved the people by defeating a dreaded enemy while risking his own life on the field of battle. Such heroes, especially if they are also just and perhaps even merciful to defeated foes, are revered, respected, and even, in a sense, worshiped as saviors. The fact that power over "creation and abolition, forgiveness and punishment," now rests with the good god Marduk, and not the gods who so quickly plotted great evil, Apsu and Tiamat, is reason for genuine celebration and gratitude.

Marduk is the model warrior king, and he stands as a strong bulwark before the ever-present threat of chaos and evil. So it is natural for the narrative to expect him to be revered, respected, and even, in a sense, worshiped as the savior of the people. We are not Marduk's beloved children, but we are his subjects and his creation, and we should be grateful that he is a god of order and goodness. While the future is open, then, gratitude and submission are called for today, and the narrative suggests that right worship, work, and the support of the people will help to ensure that Marduk's good reign will endure.

THE ABOVE NARRATIVE, which was read aloud (and perhaps enacted) for the people on the fourth day of the annual New Year's Festival in Babylon, shrewdly invokes a lively, dramatic, and easily remembered tale of the gods that subtly but powerfully urges popular obedience to and support for the monarch and the priests (p. 231). Just as the gods are to revere and to teach their children to revere Marduk, the ancient Babylonians are to revere and to teach their children to revere both Marduk and their human sovereign. The narrative, however, is not blindly subservient to power and the status quo. Marduk, the powerful and cunning sovereign, is also merciful, like a shepherd to humans, and concerned that his divine subjects might have rest. Thus Marduk represents a powerful ideal and measure for all human sovereigns, who should likewise be good, powerful, cunning, merciful, and — like good shepherds — interested in the people having rest from their labors.

The command that the people keep the shrines of Marduk is very significant in this regard, for it sets up a political power structure separate from the crown, a structure whose primary loyalty is to the good. Therefore, the call to care for the shrines and the priests who maintain them very concretely and visibly makes the power and legitimacy of human sovereigns relative to those sovereigns' fidelity to the example of Marduk. Thus the narrative provides a political base and an ethical rationale for deposing any monarch who is not good as Marduk is good. Such an evil monarch could be said to represent the return of Tiamat. And such a monarch may need to be dealt with as Marduk dealt with Tiamat. In any case, because it specifies that Marduk is good, and because it establishes a priestly power structure, a power structure separate from the crown, a power structure that is charged with remembering Marduk (i.e., remembering what is good, just, and merciful in personal and public affairs), this narrative is not a sheer paean to power and does not urge blind support of just any status quo.

In sum, the Enuma Elish advises the Babylonians to consider the good work of the gods and of human priests and sovereigns, to remember the lurking chaos, and to be thankful for prevailing order in creation and society. Whatever one's lot, one should do all one can to support the orders of creation and of society. If you are a farmer, do not be surprised that you only bring a harvest through the sweat of your brow, for you are part of the struggle against forces of disorder and decay. Work hard and be thankful that there is order enough so that with hard work you can bring home some harvest. If you are the sovereign, then follow the example of Marduk. Do not be like Tiamat. Be strong and cunning, yes, but also be merciful even to your enemies (once they are defeated), and look after your people like a good shepherd. Priests, remember the example of Marduk. Remind people and sovereigns alike of what is orderly, good, and merciful.

There is no naïve idealism in the Enuma Elish, for the earth is made up of Tiamat and people are made up of Qingu. That is, both the earth and we humans are made out of gods (Tiamat and Qingu) who could be ordered or chaotic, good or evil, and who at the time of their deaths had set themselves on a course of chaos and violence. So it is essential for rulers, priests, and all the people to be continually reminded of the teachings of the Enuma Elish and to remember their call to respect and to serve what is orderly and productive in society and creation. For if everyone fulfills the duties to which they are called in their respective roles (let us not forget the oppressive sexism powerfully embedded herein), if they keep those who tend toward evil from upsetting good order in nature and civilization, if all remember the good and the example of Marduk — then Marduk's reign (i.e., civilization) will endure, and Tiamat (chaos) will be held at bay.[3]

That is the Enuma Elish in a nutshell, the creation narrative of the ancient Babylonians, the major competing creation narrative when the primeval history of Genesis was redacted into its current form. I turn now to *Leviathan* in order to clarify the basic parameters of the modern Western Hobbesian/Darwinian creation narrative.

3. In ancient narratives generally, "chaos" is "evil" insofar as it tends to harm life, and "order" is "good" insofar as it tends to favor life. Today one may conclude that some forms of chaos favor life, and thus are good, while some forms of order are detrimental to life, and thus bad. On the whole, however, the ancient insight remains accurate. Also, as I have already mentioned but it is worth mentioning again, the Enuma Elish supports sexist power structures.

CHAPTER THREE

Leviathan

....

The Modern Western Counterpoint

1. The Predominant "Secular"
Creation Narrative of the Modern West

In the modern West, the creation narrative that offers the most influential alternative to the primeval history of Genesis is the creation narrative of materialism. It is worth repeating Daniel Dennett's succinct summary of materialism from chapter 1 above:

> *materialism:* there is only one sort of stuff, namely *matter* — the physical stuff of physics, chemistry, and physiology — and the mind is somehow nothing but a physical phenomenon. In short, the mind is the brain. According to the materialists, we can (in principle!) account for every mental phenomenon using the same physical principles, laws, and raw materials that suffice to explain radioactivity, continental drift, photosynthesis, reproduction, nutrition, and growth. It is one of the main burdens of this book to explain consciousness without ever giving in to the siren song of dualism.[1]

In popular culture the materialist creation narrative is commonly called Darwinism. While Darwin played a pivotal role in legitimating materialism, however, the essentials of materialism were in place and

---

1. Daniel Dennett, *Consciousness Explained* (New York: Back Bay Books, 1991), p. 33.

influential long before his book *The Origin of the Species by Means of Natural Selection, or The Preservation of Favored Races in the Struggle for Life* was published in 1859.[2] Darwin is significant with respect to the modern West's secular creation narrative, not because he originated it, but because he plugged a final, gaping hole in it. Advocates of materialism had concluded long before Darwin that the prime challenge to materialism's claim to provide a total explanation of reality was the amazing biological complexity that had, according to the materialist explanation of the time, *incomprehensibly* emerged within a world that was ultimately a procession of interactions among blind forces of nature.

I say "*incomprehensibly* emerged" because even prominent eighteenth-century atheists such as David Hume acknowledged that no one had offered a convincing natural explanation for biological complexity. Darwin's accomplishment was to make the complexity comprehensible by proposing a plausible, wholly natural explanation for it, thereby answering a hitherto vexing challenge. The role that Darwinism played in the history of materialism explains why in the late twentieth century, Richard Dawkins, the acclaimed Oxford evolutionary theorist and ardent atheist, would look back and gratefully say that, while it was possible to be an atheist before Darwin, "Darwin made it possible to be an intellectually fulfilled atheist," for Darwin filled the gaping hole in the materialist account.[3]

When Dawkins relates Darwin directly to atheism, however, he conflates science and metaphysics, or cosmology. That is, he is forwarding a creation narrative that asks and answers spiritual and moral questions that are beyond the ken of science. A shift from science to metaphysics is in play whenever a direct comparison is set up between evolutionary theory and any creation narrative. So materialism is in play as soon as the issue of biological complexity is seen as spiritually significant. This applies not only to atheists like Dawkins, who think the success of evolutionary theory vindicates atheism; it also applies to creationists and intelligent-design theorists who argue that the purported failure of evolutionary theory

2. Darwin, *The Origin of the Species by Means of Natural Selection, or The Preservation of Favored Races in the Struggle for Life* (New York: Random House, 1993).

3. Richard Dawkins, *The Blind Watchmaker: Why the Evidence of Evolution Reveals a Universe without Design* (New York: Norton, 1986), p. 6.

provides evidence for the existence of God. When creationists advance scientific arguments for the existence of God, they, too, conflate science and metaphysics in a confusing way. In any case, when *I* reject Dawkins's materialism, I am not rejecting the science of evolution. And if evolutionary theory were disproven, *I* would not see that as spiritually significant, but only as the reopening of a challenging scientific question about the natural development of biological complexity.

As I have argued, one can accept the spiritual truths of the Genesis Creation narratives, reject materialism, and still affirm (as I would) that contemporary evolutionary theory provides the best (if still incomplete) answer to strictly biological/scientific questions about the development of life on earth. Nowhere in my argument will I question the merits of evolutionary theory insofar as it is considered within the boundaries of science. The problem is not with science, but with materialism. Scientific argument is essential for understanding Creation, but it is methodologically incapable of discerning moral or spiritual reality or of engaging in ethical reflection.

As long as the distinction between science and metaphysics/cosmology/Creation narratives is made clear and respected, there is no cause for conflict between science and spirituality. Unfortunately, as Dawkins illustrates, the boundary between science and materialism has been neither made clear nor respected within predominant streams of modern Western reflection. Within those streams of reflection, with Darwinism typically to the fore, and often with an illicit claim to objectivity and value-neutrality running interference, the materialist creation narrative has been surreptitiously advanced as a scientific conclusion. As a result, it is easy for people to think that rejecting materialism is the same thing as rejecting science. But I am not rejecting science (e.g., I am not rejecting any discovery of physics, chemistry, biology, sociology, history, economics and all the rest); I am defending the Flood and seven-days-of-Creation narratives, and even to a degree the Enuma Elish, against modernity's major alternative cosmology, that is, the materialist narrative of Hobbesian/Darwinism. The essentials of twenty-first-century materialism were already clear in *Leviathan*, the celebrated work by seventeenth-century political philosopher Thomas Hobbes.

2. Thomas Hobbes: *Leviathan*

Leviathan (published in 1651) is a powerful defense of monarchical government that Hobbes wrote amidst the bloody English civil war. In comparison to influential seventeenth-century contemporaries such as René Descartes (the "father of modern philosophy"), Hobbes's influence on mainstream intellectual traditions in the eighteenth and nineteenth centuries was marginal. Hobbes's thought became ascendant in the twentieth century (as Descartes's star faded), for Hobbes had already in the seventeenth century anticipated the philosophical materialism that would become predominant among intellectuals in the twentieth century (and, so far, in the twenty-first century).

Because Hobbes wrote in a day in which it was important to retain traditional moral categories, he explicitly redefined key moral and spiritual concepts as they could — and in large part would — be thought within materialist boundaries. While Hobbes is not as sophisticated as his twentieth-century heirs would be, the essentials and implications of twentieth-century materialism are already fully realized in his work. As a result, Hobbes is both an especially accessible and an accurate source to use as we sketch out essential features of the modern West's materialist creation narrative.

There is no neutral argument to which materialism can appeal to demonstrate its truth, but many modern defenders of materialism seem truly to believe that their metaphysics (i.e., philosophical materialism) and their position on morality, ethics, and religion is an objective and neutral matter of scientific fact. Perhaps because he is one of the originators of materialism, Hobbes was not captured by the illusion that his position was objective and neutral. Hobbes frankly acknowledges that the strength of any argument about the ultimate character of reality can only be proportionate to the degree to which, in light of our own reflection and experience, we are led to conclude that that argument is not only accurate but also exhaustive.[4]

Realizing that materialism cannot ground itself, Hobbes acknowl-

---

4. Of course, "experience" and "reality" here must not be confined within physical, empirical bounds, for that would beg all the critical questions.

edges that each reader will have to decide, in light of the whole of his or her own life experience, whether or not his (i.e., Hobbes's) account is adequate. After "I have set down my own reading" of the character of existence "perspicuously" and in an "orderly" fashion, says Hobbes, it is only left for the reader, "to consider, if he also find not the same in himself. For this kind of Doctrine, admitteth no other Demonstration."[5] Of course, Hobbes is sure that all reasonable readers who are honest with themselves will be convinced by his account. And Hobbes's confidence has been on the whole vindicated among late twentieth- and early twenty-first-century Western intellectuals.

3. Hobbes on the Character of Reality and Our Knowledge of It

For Hobbes — as well as for twenty-first-century materialism — existence is wholly physical, a blind interplay of forces. Humans find themselves in the midst of this material existence, and whatever knowledge they have of it comes through their five senses. So the beginning of all understanding, the ultimate origin of every human idea, lies in sense impression. There is "no conception in a man's mind, which hath not at first, totally, or by parts, been begotten upon the organs of Sense" (p. 3).

We alone among the animals have not merely sensations but ideas in our minds, because we alone have the capacity for language and reasoning. We organize our sense impressions, give various objects and forces names, and we reason by observing, remembering, and ordering the relationships among the names. When our reasoning is sufficient to understand causal relationships among various names, so that we can predict what will happen when the forces/objects represented by various names interact, then we are engaging in science. In accord with the sensory sources of all ideas and our capacity to reason, Hobbes distinguishes two kinds of knowledge: "Knowledge of Fact" and "Knowledge of the Consequence of one Affirmation to another," that is, "Science" (p. 41).

To be sure, we have many ideas of fantastic beings and occult causes

---

5. Thomas Hobbes, *The Leviathan* (Amherst, NY: Prometheus Books, 1982), p. 2. Hereafter, page references to this work appear in parentheses within the text.

that are neither factual nor scientific. But all of these ideas are originally rooted in sense impressions. With regard to matters of fact, such fantastic ideas result from mixing pieces of ideas without rigorous attention to the lines of connection between ideas and sense impressions. Thus, for instance, one may mix the legitimate ideas of a woman and a fish to come up with the fantastic idea of a mermaid. Similarly, fantastic beliefs about occult causes (e.g., to see a connection between sin and lightning) stem from hasty speculation when there is ignorance of true causes, or from a failure to test and reason rigorously from our experience when determining relationships among ideas/objects.

To reiterate, the world is wholly physical for Hobbes, all knowledge originates in sense impressions, and there are only two valid kinds of knowledge: knowledge of fact and of science. Note well that once this simple set of premises is accepted — and these premises came to be seen by predominant twentieth-century intellectuals as unquestionable — wholesale materialism simply follows, and any reasonable creation narrative will have to fall within materialist parameters. It is critical to remember that there is no objective argument for materialism. Hobbes was right that the strength of any argument about the ultimate character of reality can only be proportionate to the degree to which, in light of one's own reflection and experience, one is led to conclude that that argument is not only accurate but also exhaustive.

In the end I will contend that, on precisely these grounds, my reading of the Creation and Flood narratives of Genesis concerning moral reality and of the character of love, beauty, good, and evil offers an account of reality that is far more complete, perspicuous, and accurate than that offered by materialism. Like Hobbes, accordingly, I expect reasonable readers to acknowledge that the Genesis cosmology is just as reasonable, even more complete, and so more accurate than either the Enuma Elish or Hobbesian/Darwinian cosmology.

4. Hobbes on God, Our Knowledge of God, and Causation

Hobbes does affirm the existence of God. Indeed, he affirms a version of the so-called cosmological argument for the existence of God. Namely, we

35

can conclude that at the beginning of the chain of causes that we observe in our world, there has to have been a first, originating cause, and that is God (p. 53). It is crucial, however, to track precisely what Hobbes means by "God."

Hobbes is already using "cause" here in a wholly modern, naturalistic, mechanistic sense. In Hobbes's day, when people spoke of "cause" with regard to God or creatures, they thought of "cause" in the fourfold sense that Aristotle and Saint Thomas Aquinas did. They presumed that "cause" referred to intentions, goals, materials, and effective activity. For instance, if you ask me what is the cause of the hot chocolate I made, my answer includes the fact that my kids love hot chocolate, that I love my kids, that I wanted to make them happy, that I had chocolate, milk, and a heat source available to me, and that I properly prepared the recipe. To talk about God as "first cause" of the world, then, was to talk about God's love, character, intentions, reasons, and activity. Indeed, even today many people think of cause in this rich and full way when they are thinking in terms of the causes of human actions.

For Hobbes, by contrast, "cause" means *only* a motion that produces a subsequent motion, like the thunderclap that starts the avalanche. When Hobbes says that we can know that there must be a first cause, and that that first cause is God, "God" refers to the original motion from which all subsequent motions flow (e.g., "initial conditions" plus "Big Bang" equals "God"). Insofar as Hobbes's God is first cause in this modern sense, Hobbes's God has no more love, intentions, feelings, reasons, or ongoing relationship to the world than a thunderclap has to the avalanche it sets off.

Moreover, Hobbes argues that precisely because God is infinite, it is impossible for us, whose ideas are all finite, to have any definite ideas about God beyond the bare notion of first cause. For, again, according to Hobbes's account, human knowledge is all ultimately derived from sense impressions and thus is limited to facts and science. So, while we can infer that there must be a first cause in the naturalistic sense, "which men call God," we can "not have an Idea, or Image of him," in our minds. When we speak of God in right accord with our capacities, then, we "must either use such Negative Attributes, as *Infinite, Eternall, Incomprehensible*; or Superlatives, as *Most High, most Great*, and the like; or Indefinite, as *Good, Just,*

Holy, Creator" (p. 194). Notably, Hobbes means "Indefinite" in the strongest imaginable sense, which is to say, "Indefinite" terms are wholly empty of content, as are "Negative Attributes."

Confusion about what is possible for us to say about God, Hobbes contends, leads to incoherence. For instance, theologians constantly use words that are not rigorously linked to sense impressions. As a result, their words are incoherent, for they "are without any thing correspondent to them in the mind" (p. 40). Definite theological ideas are fantastic phantasms derived from the undisciplined combination of pieces of legitimate ideas. For instance, the idea of "God incarnate," though far more complex, would be in the same category as the idea of "mermaid." Hobbes dares his reader to "see if he can translate any one chapter concerning any difficult point; as the Trinity; the Deity; the nature of Christ; Transubstantiation; Free-will, *&c.* into any of the modern tongues, so as to make the same intelligible" (p. 40). "When men write whole volumes of such stuffe," Hobbes exclaims, "are they not Mad, or intend to make others so?" (p. 40). Thus, while Hobbes does not deny the existence of God outright, he so delimits what we can know of God that it impossible for us to move from God to any concrete doctrine, law, or ethic. (Remember that, for Hobbes, even the meaning of "good" is "indefinite," which is to say, "devoid of content.")

Hobbes's strategy here is remarkably similar to the late twentieth-century "two magisteria" approach of Harvard paleontologist and evolutionary biologist Stephen Jay Gould.[6] Gould proposed a détente between religion and science based on the recognition of two distinct magisteria, the natural (the sphere of science) and the supernatural (the sphere of religion). Gould's détente appears to be innocent. Within the realm of the "natural," however, he includes not only all natural objects and nonhuman animals, but also all humans and all human capacities and artifacts (e.g., thinking, ideas, cultures, religions, anything that appears in the world). Thus, while he grants the possible existence of God and sphere of the supernatural, there is no definite or discernible connection between it and any object, idea, or force in our world. Gould shares Hobbes's opinion concerning the sensory origins of all knowledge, and thus he shares

---

6. Stephen Jay Gould, *Rock of Ages: Science and Religion in the Fullness of Life* (New York: Ballantine Books, 1999), see esp. pp. 47-96.

Hobbes's opinion of the character of any reality we might know, and thus he similarly delimits all possible human knowledge to knowledge of facts and science.

5. Hobbes on the Character of Humans

For Hobbes there are only two kinds of knowledge: of fact and of science. But why do we remember facts? Why do we work at science? For Hobbes, the answer is that we are full of desires and aversions, and our capacity to know facts and to do science greatly enhances our power to get what we desire and to avoid what we dislike. Because of our capacity to reason, we — unlike other parts of existence — possess two types of motion; like other parts of existence, we possess "vital" motion (e.g., breathing, blood flowing through our veins, food digestion, etc.); but because we can form ideas and reason, we also possess "voluntary" motion, motion that follows on a *thought* of some thing.

All voluntary motion (including thinking) is motivated by our desires and aversions and is determined in relation to our factual and scientific knowledge as we strive to move toward what we desire and to avoid what we dislike. For Hobbes, this motivational relationship among voluntary action, aversions, and desires has the status of an inviolable, universal law: "[O]f the voluntary acts of every man, the object is some *Good to himselfe*" (p. 68).[7] The reader should note that "good" and "evil" are not originally applicable to any event or action in and of itself. "Good" and "evil" are originally defined in terms of an individual's desires and aversions.

Insofar as different individuals may desire or dislike different things, what is "good" or "evil" may vary from individual to individual. In other words, in a wholly material world, "good" and "evil" do not exist apart from the desires and dislikes of various individuals (p. 24). Good and evil, then, are wholly personal and aesthetic realities. They are not yet *ethical* realities because they do not yet name anything beyond the immediate and diverse desires and aversions of individuals. For Hobbes, good and evil

7. Hobbes later specifies that "no man can transferre, or lay down his Right to save himselfe from Death, Wounds, and Imprisonment" (p. 72).

can emerge as ethical realities (i.e., as something shared above and beyond immediate personal preference) only insofar as humans have reached a social consensus that requires them to submit themselves to common standards of good and evil.

Therefore, good and evil are not part of the ultimate character of reality, because ultimately reality is simply a mechanized, brute, physical process. Only insofar as sentient beings exist do likes and dislikes, pleasures and pains, and good and evil — as ways of naming one's desires and aversions — exist. Hence, morality in the classic and ordinary sense is literally not thinkable, and the same holds for altruistic or loving action in the classic or ordinary sense. For Hobbes, no action is ever done in response to having been seized by love for any other. The object of every action is some good for oneself. Accordingly, in a radical departure from classic understanding, Hobbes identifies love wholly with desire. There is no difference, then, between one's love of justice and one's love of ice cream. Both loves are ultimately expressions of personal desire whose ultimate object and motivation is some good for oneself. And again, at its root, "good" is nothing more than the name we give to what we love, and "evil" is the name we give to what we hate. "So that," Hobbes makes clear, "Desire, and Love, are the same thing" (p. 24).

Thus, all action (i.e., voluntary motion) is necessarily selfish and is action in pursuit of one's own desires, one's own good. One can draw a distinction between self-interest and enlightened self-interest, but it is confused and unrealistic to make any appeal beyond self-interest. There is nothing that is good and lovely that is not good and lovely *for me*. Hobbes realizes that his materialist premises dictate that all ethical ideas will need to be rearticulated in terms of self-interest, and he takes care to provide these new definitions. For instance, he defines "pity" as grief "for the Calamity of another." But, he is careful to add, pity ultimately stems from self-interest because it "ariseth from the imagination that the like calamity may befall" oneself (p. 28). Pity for another, then, is really a form of concern for oneself (today we might interpret such seemingly altruistic dynamics in terms of "kinship altruism" or "reciprocal altruism").

Hobbes's materialist understanding of human character allows him to generalize about the basic driving force that drives all human action: the "object of man's desire, is not to enjoy once onely, and for one instant of time; but to assure for ever, the way of his future desire" (p. 49). As a result, until we have secured sufficient power over and against nature, and over and against all other people, to ensure that we will be able to gain whatever we desire, every person is above all consumed with "a perpetuall and restlesse desire of Power after power, that ceaseth onely in Death" (p. 49).

It is now clear why Hobbes's overarching concern in *Leviathan* is to provide a rationale for commonwealths. It is because the unmitigated, competitive, and universal quest for "Power after power" among selfish agents, which is for him the basic human reality, is a recipe for chaos. The English civil war made the horrors of such chaos visceral for Hobbes. The problem, as Hobbes discerns, is that once materialist premises are accepted, the argument for commonwealths must be made in wholly selfish terms. One cannot, for instance, appeal to any "self-evident" truth that "all men are created equal" with "rights" to "life, liberty, and the pursuit of happiness" (as one could with the moral realism that characterized the Cartesian/Lockean philosophical trajectory, which remained predominant in Western thought through the late nineteenth century). Given every person's quest for "Power after power," and given every person's pursuit of his or her desires in an amoral world, the ethical question becomes: Why would anyone want to subordinate personal preferences and affirm and support a commonwealth that sustains and enforces shared standards of good and evil, most likely against many of one's own immediate personal desires?

In the past, Hobbes contends, the challenge of justifying commonwealths was met through the invention of religion. Individual hope of gaining divine favor and fear of divine judgment made people desirous of obeying laws and sustaining commonwealths (p. 57). To some degree, Hobbes concedes, religions were invented to secure the power and prosperity of the inventors. Admittedly, indeed, the vast majority of believers ("the more ignorant sort") literally believed in fantastic religious realities. In short, Hobbes considers that religions have always traded on people's hopes and fears, in combination with their lack of understanding of what really exists (i.e., of fact) and of what really causes what in the world (i.e., of science). But Hobbes retains a generous spirit toward religions, for insofar as religions have helped to create commonwealths, they have been useful illusions (p. 57; see also p. 59).

Hobbes concludes, however, that we neither can (for much longer) nor should rely on illusions. For with the advent of modern thought, Hobbes (anticipating Freud by several centuries) judges the future of these illusions to be dim. We need a rationale for legitimating commonwealths that is wholly consistent with modernity's discovery of the true (i.e., for Hobbes, the materialist) character of reality, a reality in which there is no god, no love in the classic sense (e.g., in the sense of *hesed*, agape, or altruism), and in which there is good (what is desired) or evil (what is hateful) only in the preferential sense: for example, in the sense of desire or eros, but never in the classic moral sense.

6. The State of Nature and the Social Contract

Hobbes thinks that the reason every person should support whatever commonwealth he or she lives in becomes clear when we delineate the condition of humans who live apart from commonwealths, who live in the "state of nature." Humans who live in the state of nature are subject only to the laws of nature. Again, for Hobbes it is simple fact — and thus "the right of nature" — that each human always pursues his or her own good, which is first and foremost the pursuit of personal survival, and secondarily the pursuit of security and pleasure (p. 66).

In the state of nature, moreover, there is as yet no ethics, no right or wrong, no legal or illegal, no just or unjust — indeed, there is nothing higher than individual desire. "Good" names what someone loves, "evil" what someone hates. Moreover, in the state of nature the "right of nature" includes the natural claim every person has "to every thing; even to one anothers body" (p. 67). So when people live in the state of nature, that is, when they live apart from any commonwealth, "they are in that condition which is called Warre; and such a warre, as is of every man against every man" (p. 64). Hobbes does not mince words: "The notions of Right and Wrong, Justice and Injustice have [i.e., in the state of nature] no place. Where there is no common Power, there is no Law: where no Law, no Injustice. Force, and Fraud, are in warre the two Cardinal vertues" (p. 66).

In this state of war of all against all, no persons or clans will be powerful enough to consistently secure themselves against all others. In this state of war, moreover, human life will be primitive, for there will be insufficient stability to support the emergence of culture, industry, trade, the professions, or science (p. 65). In short, human life in the state of nature, a taste of which we get when societies disintegrate into civil war or ethnic conflict, is horrible; it is a primitive life full of "continuall feare, and danger of violent death," it is a life which is "solitary, poore, nasty, brutish, and short" (p. 65). Indeed, the horrors of human existence in the state of nature are so severe that even a peasant suffering under tyranny should prefer that commonwealth, even if it is tyrannical, to life in the state of nature.

All of this sets up Hobbes's fundamental argument for commonwealths. Since in the state of war "there can be no security to any man (how strong or wise soever he be)," it follows "that every man, ought to endeavor Peace, as farre as he has hope of obtaining it." Since this reasoning goes to the most fundamental self-interested good and is had in common by every person, Hobbes holds that it is "the first, and Fundamental Law of Nature." From this follows a second law: it is that everyone should, in the interest of securing peace, be willing to lay down his or her right to all things "and be contented with so much liberty against other men, as he would allow other men against himselfe" (in more familiar terms: my rights end where yours begin) (p. 67). This is the linchpin of the social covenant, or social contract; and in the face of this basic contract, "good" and "evil" first come into existence. That is, only in the wake of this basic contract can what is just or unjust, or what is legal or illegal, first be created (p. 82).

The existence of a social contract, then, is the *sole* basis for all ethical/moral/legal understanding. For instance, "injustice" now has content: it is the failure to fulfill a contract as it is defined within the boundaries of whatever commonwealth we find ourselves in. Justice, on the other hand, is the performance of a contract in accord with the rules of some commonwealth. Notably, *any* action performed apart from a contract is immune to condemnation, for "injustice" is limited to the failure to fulfill a contract (p. 74). If there is no contract, there is no possibility of injustice. In colloquial terms, if there is no law against something, it cannot possibly be wrong, evil, or unjust, because "wrong," "evil" and "unjust" exist only as ethical realities in the light of a contract. For example, killing another person only becomes wrong when a social contract prohibits it (i.e., when it becomes illegal). Therefore, there are no inalienable rights, for there is no moral reality — indeed, no "rights" until they are established by the social contract.

Hobbes redefines other significant concepts accordingly. For instance, "forgiveness" is being released from a contract without fulfilling its terms (of course, one forgives only if forgiving is in one's own best interests). "Gift," or "grace," is also radically redefined. When one gives something or does something for someone else without the security of an explicit, legally binding contract, but in the *hope* of gaining something, it is a gift, or a gracious action (p. 69).

This is a radical departure from the classic philosophical and religious understanding of forgiveness, gift, and grace, for in the classic understanding, the ultimate motivation is most definitely not selfish, whereas for Hobbes, selfishness is the only possible motivation for any giving or forgiving: "[N]o man giveth, but with intention of Good to himselfe; because Gift is Voluntary; and of all Voluntary Acts, the Object is to every man his own Good; of which if men see they shall be frustrated, there will be no beginning of benevolence or trust; nor consequently of mutuall help; nor of reconciliation of one man to another" (p. 78). In short, for Hobbes, unmitigated selfishness is universal, and is at the root of every human action. Therefore, all classic moral and spiritual categories must be redefined accordingly or, if that proves impossible, excised.

7. *Leviathan*

While Hobbes thinks it's crucial to provide a rational justification for commonwealths within materialist parameters, he is realistic enough to see that an appeal to reason will not carry the day in real life. The problem is that the rationale for commonwealths trades on enlightened self-interest, but these enlightened priorities are contrary to the immediate impulses of our natural passions, which "carry us to Partiality, Pride, Revenge, and the Like" (p. 87).

It would be naïve, says Hobbes, to expect that societal enlightenment and delineation of the logic of the social contract could tame our natural passions. Covenants that are "without the Sword" are but so many words, "and of no strength to secure a man at all" (p. 87). And the "bonds of words" are "too weak to bridle mens ambition, avarice, anger, and other Passions" *unless* there is "feare of some coercive Power" (p. 71). People will live in a state of war unless they live with "a common Power to keep them all in awe" (p. 64). For the "Passions that encline men to Peace," Hobbes believes, "are Feare of Death; Desire of such things as are necessary to commodious living; and a Hope by their Industry to obtain them" (p. 66).

Commonwealths are a means to more commodious living and provide the context within which industry should lead to reward. Ultimately, however, the "Passion to be reckoned upon, is Fear" (p. 73). The commonwealths' powers over life, death, and imprisonment must be awesome enough to keep people in awe and faithful to the rule of law. Thus can peace be established only insofar as the commonwealth — be it a monarchy or an assembly — is a "great Leviathan," which has "the use of so much Power and Strength" that, "by terror thereof," it is able to shape the will of all people "to Peace at home, and mutual ayd against their enemies abroad" (pp. 89-90). Hobbes provides the logic that justifies the Leviathan, but it is the fearsomeness of the Leviathan, not Hobbes's justifications, that can in fact shift us from the state of war to the state of peace.

8. Hobbes's Bleak Vision

For Hobbes, ultimate and original reality is nothing more than the state of nature, the state of war of every one against every other. While this was a radical new idea in the seventeenth century, it had become a familiar image by the end of the nineteenth century: creatures engaged in a struggle for existence that is red in tooth and claw, the natural state in which self-interest — and above all interest in survival — is ultimate. Since this is the natural state, and since there is no other reality (e.g., no moral or spiritual reality), the emergence of morality, ethics, communities and an ordered society can have nothing to do with a response to moral reality, or with cultivation and institutionalizing of the good, the just, and the loving, for in the state of nature there simply is no morality or ethics, no good or evil, no love, no just or unjust, no spirituality. There are only individuals in selfish pursuit of what they happen to desire, and in unending pursuit of the power to maximize their security and to maximize their ability forevermore to avoid aversions and to secure pleasures.

The emergence of law and justice does not signal any shift in character or recognition of a moral realm. The emergence of law and justice, of the state of peace, can only originate from some permutation of selfish pursuit — from an enlightened selfishness, to be sure, but from selfishness nonetheless. So the passions that inspire us to create the means whereby we can transcend the natural state of war and enter into a state of peace cannot be moral or spiritual passions. They cannot — for Hobbes or for materialists — involve altruism, a having been seized by love for others, a having-been-seized that motivates justice, mercy, and charity. For according to Hobbes's materialist premises, such love cannot but be a delusion. There is no change, and no change is possible, in the character or spirituality of people, for there are no moral or spiritual realities in the classic sense.

Given Hobbes's materialist presuppositions about the sources and character of our knowledge, his radical delimitation of possible talk about God (which renders even the ideas of good and justice with respect to God wholly "indefinite") does indeed follow. In this respect, I agree with Hobbes and Gould. That is, I agree that science cannot reason its way to, or even discern moral or spiritual realities as such. I do not contest, then, the impossibility of speaking coherently about morality and spirituality once we accept materialist premises. I reject materialist premises. I accept modern science, but I reject materialism insofar as I do not agree that the parameters of modern science circumscribe the parameters of reality, for, quite reasonably, I take account both of sense impressions and of having been seized by love for others, by grace, by the love of God.

I reject Hobbes because I find his account — most notably his denial of the reality of our having been seized by love for others — utterly unbelievable. Hobbes's vision of reality is dark and depressing, and one can be thankful that, despite its ongoing predominance within Western thought in its updated, neo-Darwinian form, there is no good reason for reasonable people to affirm it as true.[8]

8. Note that, despite all the euphemistic talk of "selfish genes," "cooperative" genes, "kinship altruism," and such, there is no space in evolutionary theory for morality, altruism, or spirituality in the ordinary and classic moral and spiritual senses. Everything is ultimately indexed to and defined in terms of evolutionary potentials,

Unfortunately, insofar as Darwinism has been functioning in the modern West not simply as a well-established scientific theory about how species evolved or as the best scientific trajectory along which to investigate the origins of life within the cosmos (to be clear, I affirm evolutionary theory in these regards), but as a metaphysics/cosmology that — together with the other modern sciences — wholly addresses and explains all reality, modern secular society has largely if unwittingly embraced the amoral Hobbesian/Darwinian vision of reality as its de facto creation narrative.

This is unfortunate because, considered morally as a creation narrative, the Hobbesian/Darwinian vision represents a step backward even from the Enuma Elish, which embodies the realpolitik of the Hobbesian/Darwinian account without denying and undercutting the moral realm. According to the materialist version, our moral and spiritual apprehensions are illusory. While there may be (in a metaphorical sense) both "selfish genes" and "cooperative genes" — it would be helpful when engaging in biology to speak strictly in terms of parasitic and symbiotic interactions — reality does not, at root, distinguish among genes morally, and ultimately there are no moral forces in nature, and there is no reality beyond nature (i.e., where "nature" is understood in the modern materialist sense). Our most profound moral apprehensions are real only in a secondary, epiphenomenal sense. That is, we really do feel them; but they are nonetheless not what we suppose them to be. For they do not reflect any reality, they do not respond to anything that is really "out there," outside our own minds, feelings, and social constructions. On the materialist account, our moral feelings are wholly a function of our genetic inheritance and our conditioning.

When Darwinism is taken not merely as a scientific theory about an aspect of reality but as a total theory, as a cosmology, our most profound moral apprehensions must be interpreted as products of the ways in which our brains have been programmed and conditioned to experience certain phenomena in accord with biological and sociocultural forces (i.e., nature and nurture). It is not difficult to discern how this gives indirect support

which is to say, in terms of any trait's relationship to the potential for one gene pool or kinship group to survive.

and cover to those among us who are most immoral (i.e., since they deny moral reality). Unfortunately, modern Western society, the most technologically sophisticated and powerful society the world has ever seen, has largely adopted Darwinism not merely as a promising, if still young, biological theory, but, taken together with Hobbesian ideas, as a fully formed creation narrative.

Given the power of this totalizing modern cosmology in the background, it is not surprising to see the aesthetic sphere elide the moral, to see chasms open between what is legal and illegal on the one hand, and what is good and evil on the other, to witness massive denials of moral responsibility and blatant affirmation of good and "might makes right" mentalities, to see greed affirmed and those who are greedy and "successful" admired, and to see self-interest trumpeted as the only ultimate justification for rational action. It is not surprising to discover that brute understanding of "survival of the fittest" in "nature red in tooth and claw" is largely and disturbingly descriptive of real social relations within and among modern societies. After all, on materialist premises, what else would we expect of ourselves or others?

Unfortunately, while modern Western scholars have done good work explaining how the hierarchical character of medieval cosmology tended to reinforce hierarchical, patriarchal, and oppressive social and interfamily relationships in medieval society, they have not been as quick to note the brutal, unjust, and oppressive implications of Darwinian/Hobbesian cosmology for modern society. Taken as such an all-encompassing theory — that is, not merely as an empirical investigation into empirical phenomena but as a complete account of who and what we are and of the ultimate character of existence — a Hobbesian/Darwinian cosmology is a massively significant moral step backward even from the Enuma Elish, which affirmed the reality of good and evil.

In short, in the modern West, a Hobbesian/Darwinian cosmology is functioning as an essentially religious creation narrative, the creation narrative of the modern secular sphere, the creation narrative of materialism. Insofar as materialism has spread from the West and across the globe, this is not merely a Western but a global problem. Moreover, in the tried-and-true fashion of ideologies throughout history, materialism often illegitimately declares itself to be value-neutral, to be free of any metaphysical entanglements (the latter supposedly only afflict religions), and to be the only legitimate arbiter of any real knowledge.

Hobbes is right about human selfishness and what is often our ruthless pursuit of self-interest. The Enuma Elish, along with all of the world's classic religious traditions, also emphasizes the reality and potential severity of human selfishness. The difference lies in Hobbes's conclusion that, insofar as one can speak of ethics and ethical agents at all, "ethics" will *necessarily* have some permutation of selfishness (e.g., "enlightened self-interest/selfishness") as its primordial and ultimate driving force. For in Hobbes there simply is no moral reality in the realist sense. As a result, unfortunately, Hobbes's understanding, most notably his presumption that in fact there is no moral reality, hardens human hearts toward all other creatures (including all other humans).

I will quite reasonably and with considerable concern reject Hobbes's bleak and morally empty understanding of the character of reality. While we may disagree, however, we cannot but be stunned by the brilliance with which Hobbes saw the implications of the modern science and philosophy that was only just emerging in the middle of the sixteenth century. Moreover, Hobbes's goal is clearly admirable. In the throes of a brutal civil war, and remaining rigorously within the bounds of reality insofar as he understood it, Hobbes strove mightily to develop a reasonable rationale for organizing a civil order out of the brutal chaos of anarchy.

I disagree with Hobbes's theory, but I respect Hobbes, and I even suspect that he was moved to engage in such a difficult and potentially dangerous polemic because of his not at all selfish or self-interested sensitivity to and concern for all the suffering that surrounded him. I wonder whether or not we encounter a prototype in Hobbes: the prototype of people we should sincerely pity, of people who in their daily living are truly awake to love for others, but who, due to the degree to which they are captured by modern Western materialist rationality, suffer in their theory, in the fullness of their understanding, and in the poetic richness of their spiritual articulations.

The Hobbesian/Darwinian creation narrative, which is arguably the operative creation narrative of the predominant conceptual trajectories of modern Western rationality, is spiritually impoverished, for it elides the reality of love, good, and evil. But I have yet to map out with any precision my understanding of the Hebrew cosmology of the primeval history, to unfold its spiritual richness and, especially, to detail how it allows those who live in the wake of full-bodied affirmation of moral reality — of good and evil — to affirm themselves and reality as they live with eyes wide open to all the injustice and suffering that suffuses reality.

CHAPTER FOUR

The Genesis Flood

Shattering Violence

I promised to keep my eyes wide open to all the injustice and suffering that suffuses reality. This commitment requires me to name, right up front, three scenes of shattering violence about which the Flood narrative of Genesis pivots. First, there are the depths of human wickedness that the narrative credits with stirring God to unleash a devastating flood. Second, there is the Flood itself, a flood of such devastating violence that it is said to kill every land and air creature on earth — with the exception of the handful on the ark. The third is the smallest in scale but, I will argue, pivotal in the narrative: the bloody sacrifice Noah offers immediately after disembarking from the ark.

In the wake of the murder, the rape, the earthquake, or the tsunami, people are typically sensitive enough to avoid unnecessarily exposing devastated loved ones or even themselves to explicit descriptions of the violence, suffering, and death. This is a sensitivity that the Genesis narrative reflects. Each of the three scenes of violence is clearly named, and there is no doubting the devastating realities; but the narrative is sensitive enough to keep explicit scenes of violence offstage. Nonetheless, sheltering the consciousness we have in the twenty-first century, now far distant from the horrors of these three scenes of violence, would promote a profound misreading of the narrative. For, as we shall see, the whole point of the Flood narrative is to respond spiritually to the unimaginable horrors that permeate our world. Indeed, the Flood narrative is the locus and product of a centuries-long struggle to articulate a spiritual response to the horrors that suffuse reality.

1. The Gilgamesh Epic

There is little doubt that the Genesis Flood narrative is rooted in a historical event, because there are numerous other narratives of a devastating flood in the lore of the Ancient Near East. Those narratives appear in diverse languages and versions, and the earliest written narratives date to around 1700 BCE.[1] Some are strikingly similar to the Genesis account, our received version, which dates to around 500 BCE. For instance, in one Mesopotamian narrative, the gods sent a great flood because humans were becoming too numerous. A human, Atrahasis, saved humanity when he saved his wife and himself from destruction by building an ark. He was granted immortality as a reward for his ingenuity.[2]

The parallels to Genesis in another Mesopotamian narrative, the Gilgamesh Epic, are even more striking, and I will momentarily digress here to consider them in some detail. In the Gilgamesh Epic the gods, on the counsel of the great warrior god Enlil, resolve to wipe out humans, who have become too numerous, with a "Deluge." One of the gods, Ea, finds this decision too extreme. So Ea sends the human Uta-napisti a dream. In the dream Ea reveals the plans of the gods and instructs Uta-napisti to "demolish [or dismantle] the house, build a boat! Abandon riches and seek survival! Spurn property and save life! Put on board the boat the seed of all living creatures!"[3] Uta-napisti follows detailed instructions for building the boat and saving the seed of all living things.

The Gilgamesh Epic reports that the Deluge was awful. "Quickly it blew . . . like a battle . . . over the people. One person could not see another, nor people recognize each other in the destruction" (p. 711). Indeed, "Even the gods took fright at the Deluge!" (p. 711). They withdrew to the "heaven of Anu," where in their fright they were "curled up like dogs, lying out in the open" (p. 711). Belet-ili, who had given birth to humanity, was overcome by the sight of all the corpses. "[S]creaming like a woman in child-

---

1. Stephanie Dalley, trans. and ed., *Myths from Mesopotamia: Creation, the Flood, Gilgamesh and Others* (Oxford: Oxford University Press, 1989), p. 3.

2. Dalley, *Myths from Mesopotamia*, pp. 2-8.

3. A. R. George, *The Babylonian Gilgamesh Epic*, vol. 1 (Oxford: Oxford University Press, 2003), p. 705. Hereafter, page references to this work appear in parentheses in the text. See also Dalley's translation of this narrative, pp. 109-16.

birth," she laments that she ever agreed to the plan of the assembly of the gods to send the Deluge. "They are my people!" she exclaims, but "[now] like so many fish they fill the sea!" (p. 711). The other gods, "wet-faced with sorrow," weep with her (p. 711).

Uta-napisti, the human who had built the boat, remembers opening a porthole and seeing the awful destruction: "The Deluge ended . . . there was quiet, but all the people had turned to clay" (p. 711). Everything had been wiped away by the deluge, and "the flood plain was level like a roof." In jarring contrast to the devastation he looked upon, the skies were blue and "sunlight fell on the side of my face." Overcome, Uta-napisti recounts: "I fell to my knees and sat there weeping, the tears streaming down the side of my face" (p. 713).

Eventually, the boat comes to rest on Mount Nimus. Uta-napisti releases a dove, but it can find no place to perch, so it returns. Then he releases a swallow, which also returns. Finally, he releases a raven, and it "saw the waters receding," so it did not return (p. 713). Then Uta-napisti opens the doors of the boat, disembarks, and makes a sacrifice. And the "gods smelled the savour, the gods smelled the sweet savour, the gods gathered like flies around the sacrificer" (p. 713). When Belet-ili, the mother of humanity, arrives, she creates a "lapis lazuli necklace" and declares, with clear reference to her burning sorrow over agreeing to send the Deluge, that she will wear it so that she will "remember these days and never forget them!" (p. 715).

When Enlil, who had talked the gods into unleashing the Deluge, arrives, sees the boat, and discovers that the flood has not destroyed everything as he had planned, he is furious (p. 715). But by now the other gods, together with Belit-ili, grieve their decision to bring the Deluge. Now they agree that Ea was right all along, that the flood was a terrible mistake, and so they have sworn never to forget the horrors and the lesson learned. Ea rebukes Enlil: "You, the sage of the gods, the hero, how could you lack counsel and cause the deluge?" (p. 715). It would be just to punish the one who does wrong, Ea argues, but to react with the deluge was intemperate. If you want to reduce the population, Ea says, "let a wolf come up and diminish the people," or let a famine reduce the population, but do not wipe out everyone with a flood (p. 715).

In the end, in the wake of witnessing all the death, suffering, and horror of the flood, the gods see that Ea's decision to help Uta-napisti in saving the seed of every living thing in the boat is utterly vindicated. Apparently, even Enlil is convinced, for it is Enlil himself who goes onto the boat, takes the hands of Uta-napisti and his wife, touches their foreheads, blesses them, and makes them "gods" (p. 717).

The existence of numerous similar flood narratives suggests that, whatever the historical reality (e.g., the collapse of an ice dam, a thousand-year flood, a tsunami), the people of the Ancient Near East carried the memory of some devastating flood in their collective memory. That memory was carried in diverse and evolving oral and written traditions that, no doubt buttressed by the experience of other floods and other natural disasters over the course of generations and centuries, matured into narratives such as the Babylonian Gilgamesh Epic and the Flood narrative of the primeval history in Genesis.

At the root of the flood narratives, then, was the experience of survivors as they struggled to cope with shock, pain, and loss. The question confronting those survivors, and which confronted so many after the Indian Ocean tsunami of 2004, the earthquake in Haiti in 2010, the tsunami that struck Japan in 2011 — and which has confronted so many others in the wake of equally intense and personally devastating tragedies on scales both small and large — was this: How, now, do we live? In the face of such wrenching pain, grief, suffering, and death, what, now, are we to make of our lives? What, now, for affirming reality? What, now, for affirming ourselves?

The flood narratives are not merely reactions to a particular event. They are ancient societies' collective responses to the tragic character of existence — from volcanoes, floods, and earthquakes to death in childbirth, from snakebite, and from infection. The Genesis Flood narrative is not primarily focused on the history of a great flood. It is primarily focused on naming and responding to tragedy and to the tragic character of existence. That is, flood and creation narratives, along with other narratives about gods and cosmic powers, constitute central parts of various people's creation narratives, their cosmologies. They are meant to explain the primordial and ultimate character and meaning of reality, to put us into a picture along with other animals, gods, and cosmic powers — good and evil.

2. Spirituality, Not Science

Naturally, the Flood in the Genesis narrative presumes the science of the day. The narrative's explanation of where the waters came from is given in terms of the ancient understanding of the physical ordering of the cosmos. And that explanation is reasonable enough. Given only a basic awareness of the existence and placement of seas, rivers, wells, and rains, it is reasonable to suppose, as did the ancient Israelites, that we live on an area of dry land and air that is surrounded above (where rain comes from), below (where well water comes from), and all around (rivers and seas) by water. This is the same dry space of earth and air that God creates by separating the waters in the seven-days-of-Creation narrative.[4]

We are far past the point where it is credible to accept such primitive scientific understanding, so there is no denying that the narrative presumes ancient science that has long since become obsolete. But defending the science of the day is not the point of the narrative. Indeed, by the time "every kind of food that is eaten" is stored up in sufficient quantity to allow all on the ark to survive for a year (Gen. 6:21), and by the time all of the animals, "two by two, male and female" — peacefully and, the syntax suggests, of their own accord — "went into the ark with Noah" (Gen. 7:9), we have left the realm of science even by Ancient Near Eastern standards.[5] This departure from the scientific is no scandal because, again, the primary questions the Flood narrative addresses are not scientific or historical questions but spiritual ones. And the spiritual truth claims of this text are not affected by the demise of ancient science.

4. Unlike the two Creation narratives (i.e., the seven-days-of-Creation and the Adam-and-Eve narratives), which we receive in sequence in Genesis 1 and 2, at least two Flood traditions in Genesis have been roughly combined into a single whole (chaps. 6–9). In most English versions, the two traditions can be discerned most easily if one tracks the oscillating names for the deity (e.g., in many translations "Lord" in contrast to "God"). As with the Creation narratives, the literal inconsistencies in the combined narrative would have been obvious to the ancient Israelites. And so again, as with the first Creation narrative, the most reasonable conclusion one can draw from the inconsistencies is that they were recognized but were of no concern to those responsible for our received form of the narrative.

5. The rains lasted forty days and nights, but, according to the narrative, it was a year before anyone disembarked from the ark.

3. The Flood Narrative as Neo-Creation Narrative

Notably, the Flood narrative in Genesis is close kin to the Creation narratives in Genesis. The urgent purpose of the Flood narrative is spiritual. Moreover, the overflowing waters of the Flood are the very waters God separated in the Creation narrative in order to create the dry earth on which vegetation and creatures could live. These very waters return in the Flood to bring watery chaos over all. This marks the return of the formless and void "deep" of the seven-days-of-Creation narrative. All creatures of land and air are once again rendered formless and void. And after the Flood, these very chaotic waters are once again separated so that dry land appears. In this way, the Flood narrative is a second-order Creation narrative.

The Flood is a "second-order" Creation narrative because it differs from first-order Creation narratives in two basic respects. First, in the Flood narrative there is no radical new act of creation. In the Flood narrative, life is not created but delivered from the watery chaos. Notably, inside the ark one recognizes the peaceable creation portrayed in the seven-days-of-Creation narrative (more on the peaceable creation presently), a peaceable remnant preserved amidst the devastating waters. The ark preserves a microcosm of the peaceable creation, enough to provide for its regeneration when once again God causes dry land to appear.

Second, and far more significant, there is a stark contrast between the real world of the Flood narrative and the idyllic world of the two Genesis Creation narratives (i.e., of either the peaceable creation of the seven-days narrative or the Garden of Eden where Adam and Eve at first lived in blissful innocence). The Flood narrative of Genesis gives us the world as we know it, a world full of evil intentions, evil acts, and natural suffering. The Creation narratives, by contrast, are basically eschatological in character, describing not the world as it is, but the world as the ancient Israelites believed God would have it, the world as, in the eschatological Day of the Lord, they hoped and believed it would/will someday be (though explicit hope in a future heavenly time is not found in the primeval history).

By contrast, the Flood narrative, from its beginning (the wickedness of humanity covering the earth) to its finish (Noah's sacrifice, people and other creatures killing people, societies that practice capital punishment and actions that call forth capital punishment), portrays creation as we most decidedly find it, namely, full of love and joy but also permeated by overwhelming evil and violence. Again, as will become increasingly clear, the final redactors of the Genesis Flood narrative stand with us as we stare unblinking and in horror at all of the injustice and suffering that suffuse reality.

4. *All* Creatures and a Violent Turn

The Genesis Flood narrative specifies that, with the ark, God "remembers" (i.e., holds, keeps, protects, cares for) not only Noah and his family but also "all the wild animals and all the domestic animals" (Gen. 8:1). Moreover, the narrative specifies that God explicitly instructs Noah to bring every animal out of the ark, "so that they may abound on the earth, and be fruitful and multiply on the earth" (8:17). This remembering of all the creatures threatened by the Flood and this blessing of all the creatures on the ark repeats and expands on a blessing of the fishes and birds in the seven-days-of-Creation narrative: "God blessed them, saying, 'Be fruitful and multiply and fill the waters in the seas, and let birds multiply on the earth'" (Gen. 1:22). In the context of the Flood narrative, the parallel blessing is explicitly expanded to include "every living thing that is with you of all flesh — birds and animals and every creeping thing that creeps on the earth" (8:17). In a sweet touch, the narrative notes that the animals, most of whom famously entered the ark in twos, "went out of the ark by families" (8:19).

Immediately after recounting this happy exit from the ark, which itself offers us a wondrous picture of the peaceable creation amidst the chaotic waters, the text, without comment, moves directly to a shattering act of violence: "Then Noah built an altar to the Lord, and took of every clean animal and of every clean bird, and offered burnt offerings on the altar" (8:20). This is a violent departure from the harmony of the peaceable creation of the seven-days narrative, a violent departure from the peaceable ark, where all creatures are remembered and preserved amid chaos. And, while I will not develop the point just yet, it is worth noting that this violent act stands in stunning contrast to the vision of that eschatological day proclaimed by the prophet Isaiah, that day when "the lion will eat straw" and the "wolf will lie with the lamb" because there will be no harm done on earth, that day when "they will not hurt or destroy on all my holy mountain, for the earth will be full of the knowledge of the LORD as the waters cover the sea" (Isa. 11:6, 7, 9).

Not only does this violence stand in marked contrast to the harmony of God's peaceable creation as pictured in the seven-days-of-Creation narrative; it signals a stunning shift in Noah's way of relating to God. For this act of offering a sacrifice marks the first time in the narrative when Noah, who has remained speechless throughout, acts on his own initiative. Up to this point, Noah has taken every act in quiet obedience to divine directives; here, by contrast, Noah not only takes initiative for the first time, but in so doing he suggests, of his own initiative, what kind of covenantal relationship will structure a human relationship with God.

I will argue that Noah engages here in a twofold act of violence before God, and that this twofold act of violence marks the decisive turning point in the Flood narrative. I will also argue that God's response to Noah's violence marks the narrative climax of the Flood narrative. However, before I can discuss the signal significance of Noah's shattering act of violence and the divine response, I explicitly need to reflect on both covenant and sacrifice: and I need more fully to defend my claim that Noah's act of ritual sacrifice is a shattering act of violence.

5. Covenants (Reciprocal and Unilateral) and Sacrifice

There are two major types of covenant in Hebrew Scripture. The first is reciprocal, a matter of exchange: we humans fulfill certain requirements (e.g., offer sacrifices, keep divine commands), and, in turn, God will bless and keep us. The second type of covenant is unilateral, a sheer gift, and it involves an unconditional commitment on the part of God. With his act of sacrifice Noah is not simply taking initiative; he is taking initiative in such a way as to decide between these two kinds of covenantal relationship. In offering a sacrifice Noah proposes/presumes and seeks to instantiate the first kind of covenant, a divine/human relationship that is reciprocal.

This account of Noah's offering of a sacrifice is consistent with an ancient and well-established tradition of sacrifice in the Jewish tradition. It was part of an independent flood narrative more ancient than our received Genesis narrative, and in its original context it was most likely intended to validate both the sacrificial system and its correlate presumption that we stand in a reciprocal covenantal relationship with God.

Because of this background affirmation in Jewish tradition of sacrifice, some may suspect that I am imposing a radically alien perspective on the text when I characterize Noah's sacrifice as a shattering act of violence. After all, animal sacrifice was an established part of ancient Israelite religious practice. Indeed, animal sacrifice is a well-established and commended activity throughout Hebrew Scripture and was a central practice of Jewish Temple ritual right up to the Temple's destruction in 70 CE.

Notably, the logic of animal sacrifice is entirely consistent with love for all creatures of every kind. Because of a widespread modern eliding of nonhuman others from the sphere of rational moral concern, and the correlate denigration of the value of nonhuman lives, this consistency has not always been obvious to modern readers. It is, nevertheless, patent, for the significance of a sacrifice is directly related to one's belief that the object or subject being sacrificed has value and to how profoundly one values it.[6] Suppose I tell you that for Lent, or in order to engage in an act that publicly represents my solidarity with cancer survivors, I have given up coffee. Now, let us suppose that I, in fact, hate coffee. My giving up coffee is not much of a sacrifice, to say the least. At the other extreme, we are all immediately humbled in the face of an event where someone has sacrificed his or her very life for the sake of another.

To be perfectly plain, animal sacrifice is profoundly significant among peoples who practice it only because those peoples have a profound sense for the value of animal life. It is precisely this profound valuation of nonhuman animals that makes nonhuman animals appear to be so valuable that they are considered worthy offerings of sacrifice to the gods. If one did not value the animals, then one's animal sacrifice would be akin to my giving up coffee, more a mockery of sacrifice than an actual sacrifice.

A sacrifice is real only to the degree that it is a substantial, even a

---

6. Note that insofar as the animal (human or not) sacrificed was an unwilling victim of the ritual, I use "sacrifice" here in a very problematic way.

wrenching event. That is the spiritual logic of sacrifice. Notably, this logic of sacrifice explains why there would be a natural progression from the sacrifice of nonhuman animals to human sacrifice, extending even to the sacrifice of one's own children. The sacrifice of one's own child is the most hallowed form of sacrifice precisely because it is utterly unthinkable and horrifying. It is the sacrificing of what is absolutely most precious, where the offering up of the sacrifice is utterly wrenching.[7]

From the perspective of those who, like the ancient Israelites, confess faith in a God of love, the glaring problem with animal (including human) sacrifice, then, is not rooted in a lack of love for animals. On the contrary, the full apprehension of the value of all creatures who are sacrificed is utterly essential to the spiritual logic of sacrifice. The glaring problem comes with recognition that God is love. For it makes no sense to suppose that a God of love, a God who is offended by acts of violence and injustice toward beloved creatures, would be pleased and placated by further acts of bloody violence. Recognition of the loving character of God and thus of such awful confusion would certainly explain the vigorous critique of the practice of animal sacrifice that emerged within the ancient Hebrew community.

6. The Ancient Hebrew Critique of Sacrifice

An early manifestation of this critique, however limited, is probably revealed in the disturbing story of Abraham and Isaac (Gen. 22). In its present form, this much-debated and quite horrifying story begins with God's demanding that Abraham sacrifice his son, Isaac. In the end, an angel from the Lord stops Abraham from sacrificing Isaac, and Abraham offers a ram in Isaac's place. Whatever theological meaning this story may carry in its present context, in its earliest contexts it probably marks a positive step forward, for it most likely functioned to prohibit (and possibly to stop) the practice of human sacrifice among the ancient Israelites.

7. Interestingly, the Hebrews, like most peoples who practiced animal sacrifice, only offered domestic animals, never wild animals, for sacrifice. Consistent with the logic of sacrifice, this meant that one only ever offered animals that were a part of one's household, animals with which one had lived in a positive, caretaking relationship.

But the internal critique of sacrifice quite consistently extends beyond concern with human sacrifice. Consider, for instance, Isaiah 1:11: "'What to me is the multitude of your sacrifices?' says the Lord. 'I have had enough of burnt offerings of rams and the fat of fed beasts; I do not delight in the blood of bulls, or of lambs, or of goats.'" Precisely and exclusively, the blood of these rams, bulls, lambs, and goats is the nearest referent when a few verses later the prophet continues: "'When you stretch out your hands, I will hide my eyes from you; even though you make many prayers, I will not listen; your hands are full of blood. Wash yourselves; make yourselves clean; remove the evil of your doings from before my eyes; cease to do evil, learn to do good; seek justice, rescue the oppressed, defend the orphan, plead for the widow'" (Isa. 1:15-17). This is the same prophet who will later proclaim the coming of a day when a righteous judge will reign, when the "the wolf shall live with the lamb" and "the lion shall eat straw," when "they will not hurt or destroy on all my holy mountain, for the earth will be full of the knowledge of the Lord as the waters cover the sea" (Isa. 11:1-9).

This trajectory is taken up and reaffirmed in the later strata of tradition found in Isaiah 65. Isaiah 65:17 gives an eschatological description of the day when God will "create new heavens and a new earth." In that day, Isaiah proclaims, no infants shall die, everyone will live a full lifetime, and everyone will receive their fair share of the fruits of the earth. Moreover, the chapter concludes, "The wolf and the lamb shall feed together, the lion shall eat straw like the ox; but the serpent — its food shall be dust! They shall not hurt or destroy on all my holy mountain, says the Lord" (Isa. 65:25).

Obviously, the words "but the serpent — its food shall be dust!" strike an incongruent, vengeful note within an extended poetic description of a wholly blessed, just, and peaceable creation. This is the standard translation, and it is grammatically plausible. Moreover, this translation maintains the spirit of God's curse of the serpent in the far more ancient Eve-and-the-Serpent or Fall narrative (Gen. 3:14). But this translation and its pejorative understanding of "its food shall be dust" is jarringly incongruent with the passage's peaceable "new heavens and new earth" context and is theologically objectionable insofar as it portrays a petty God who forgives all humans and all other creatures while inexplicably clinging to and satisfying vengeance toward snakes.

More consistently, one could translate the line not as "but the serpent" but as "*and* the serpent — its food shall be dust." And one could understand the repetition of the words of the curse in this context as redemptive and consistent with the eschatological "wolf and the lamb shall feed together" theme. The ancient Israelites would have experienced serpents most dramatically in their killing of other animals and in their biting people (sometimes fatally). The fact that serpents (snakes, venomous vipers) will now eat only dust (e.g., just as worms do) would bring marked relief, for it portrays serpents taking their peaceable place in the peaceable creation. I should note that this reading of the phrase makes it analogous to the "child shall put its hand in the adder's den" line in the earlier and parallel description of God's peaceable creation in Isaiah 9.

According to this reading, the serpents — which humans (still) dread — will no longer kill. Humans will no longer need to fear the poisonous serpent lurking beside the front stoop, for "the serpent, its food shall be dust!" That is, in an unexpected but elegant poetic reversal, what once was curse ("its food shall be dust" of the more ancient Fall narrative) is now blessing. In sum, this alternative reading, now joyful, of the exclamation "and the serpent, its food shall be dust" is grammatically permissible and is far more theologically and contextually consistent than the standard reading, which portrays God as bizarrely petty and vindictive when it comes to snakes.

Notably, the warrant for reading this passage as an elegant poetic reversal is strengthened only a few verses later, when Isaiah emphasizes that the Lord looks "to the humble and contrite in spirit" (Isa. 66:2), and immediately continues with these astonishing affirmations:

> Whoever slaughters an ox is like one who kills a human being; whoever sacrifices a lamb, like one who breaks a dog's neck; whoever presents a grain offering, like one who offers swine's blood; whoever makes a memorial offering of frankincense, like one who blesses an idol. These have chosen their own ways, and in their abominations they take delight. (Isa. 66:3)

Note that here one finds not just an affirmation of the value of nonhuman animal life, and not just a rejection of the idea that God is pleased by the violence of sacrifice, but also a rejection of the idea that God is pleased by any dynamic of external offering (including even the nonviolent offering of grain and frankincense). The emphasis turns one's focus away from any action or deed, and away from reciprocal, tit-for-tat covenants. God is not focused on external actions in fulfillment of ritual demands. God looks within — "to the humble and contrite in spirit."

For many Jews and Christians, this discussion will have brought to mind an even more famous instance of this line of prophetic critique and affirmation. In a much-quoted passage, the prophet Micah asks rhetorically, "With what shall I come before the Lord?" He goes through a list of possibilities: burnt offerings; calves a year old; thousands of rams; rivers of oil; my firstborn. No. I shall come before the Lord with resolve "to do justice, and to love kindness, and to walk humbly with [my] God" (Mic. 6:8).

While I am obviously finding ways to affirm apparently problematic passages in Hebrew Scripture, shared by the Jewish and Christian traditions, I am not seeking to offer a general apologetic for these biblical passages. To the degree that any religion's scriptures affirm animal (including human) sacrifice, I reject those texts as tragically confused, as failing spiritually insofar as they do not apprehend how the character of the divine is manifest in our having been seized by love for all creatures. In the same way, I reject Jewish and Christian texts and traditions (among others) that affirm ritual animal sacrifice.

However, with regard to Hebrew Scripture, embraced by both Christians and Jews, it is significant and hardly surprising to note that they contain not only affirmations of animal sacrifice but also substantial *critiques* of animal sacrifice. Moreover, the critique is complex and profound, for it rejects not only the violence of animal sacrifice, but any relationship with God predicated on external realities that satisfy terms of exchange. As I will detail in the following chapter vis-à-vis the Flood narrative, instead of affirming a bloody tit-for-tat relationship, the scriptural critique affirms a relationship predicated on divine gift/grace that is realized in a change of spirit.

That is, in the scriptures of a community that practiced animal sacrifice, one finds not only a prophetic rejection of animal sacrifice, but a rejection of an understanding of covenant as a tit-for-tat relationship and an affirmation of divine grace as the basis of a relationship with God. What is rejected is not merely a *bloody* tit-for-tat relationship, but *any* tit-for-tat relationship at all. This prophetic critique was well established in ancient Judaism. Significantly, the Flood narrative — indeed, the received version of the entire primeval history, while it is now placed in an influential location at the very beginning of Hebrew Scripture, comes from a relatively late period in Israelite history, from a time when a critique of both animal sacrifice and a tit-for-tat covenant was well established within the Jewish prophetic tradition. [8]

7. Sacrifice in the Ancient Hebrew and the Modern Western Context

It is not uncommon to find modern Westerners smug and condescending with regard to the practice of animal sacrifice. It is not uncommon to find modern Westerners who think that we moderns are far more spiritually advanced than a culture that is engaged in ritual sacrifice of animals — like that of the ancient Israelites. There is absolutely no justification for this attitude. For, in accord with the logic of sacrifice, even those who affirmed animal sacrifice could do so only because of their profound love for every creature, could do so only because of their profound sense of the awfulness of the sacrifice, for the infinite violation of the killing, a violation of such magnitude that it can stand as significant before the gods in relation to the worst sins of the people.

The ancient Israelites were, on the whole, all in agreement that the life of every creature was sacred. It is in the modern West that nonhuman

---

8. I should probably pause to note that I would argue that Jesus was not sacrificed in the sense I am here critiquing. The killing of Jesus is not remotely portrayed in the Gospels as an act intended to placate God. To the contrary, what is affirmed is the sacrifice Jesus makes precisely as a consequence of his insistence on doing justice, loving kindness, and walking humbly with God even when that stance arouses the wrath of those whose power is threatened by his teachings. Jesus is never portrayed as one seeking to be killed; indeed, on the contrary, Jesus wants to live (see his desperate but faithful prayer at Gethsemane). Perhaps not coincidentally, the passage Jesus is reported to have cited in definition of his ministry — "The spirit of the Lord is upon me . . . he has anointed me to bring good news to the poor. He has sent me to proclaim release to the captives, and recovery of sight to the blind, to let the oppressed go free" (Luke 4:18-19) — is a quote from the beginning of Isaiah 61.

creatures have been systematically elided from our moral vision. In this respect the modern West is morally primitive in comparison to the ancient Israelites.

In stark contrast to modern culture, there are two options that are thinkable and were debated by the ancient Israelites. Either, in the first instance, there is profound respect for every creature and affirmation of sacrifice (again, unless there is love for the creature being killed, the "sacrifice," like my giving up coffee, is a sham); or, in the second instance, there is profound respect for every creature and a rejection of animal sacrifice as a bloody offense before God. The predominant modern Western option, the notion of an ontological divide that allows one to draw an absolute moral distinction between humans and other animals, a notion that allows animals to be treated as machines or utilized as humans wish whenever it is convenient for them, that notion is absolutely beyond the pale of either side in the ancient debate over animal sacrifice.

Therefore, while the question of animal sacrifice is an area of vigorous and unresolved debate among the ancient Israelites, *both those who affirmed and those who rejected animal sacrifice would have condemned* predominant modern Western understanding and treatment of nonhuman animals. Extreme practices such as trophy hunting or factory farms would have mortified all of the ancient Israelites, excepting those awful persons who "break a dog's neck" (Isa. 63, NRSV, as cited above). Indeed, in accord with the logic of sacrifice, it is clear that a society that so little respects animal lives that it tolerates factory "farms" could not possibly sacrifice animals (called "production units" by agribusiness) before the gods. In such a society the killing of animals would be too cheap an event to make it a candidate for sacrificial offering. For the same reasons, a society that practices animal sacrifice could not tolerate factory "farms." In such a society the killing of an animal would be so awesome/awful an event that it could never be done so cheaply and easily as it is done in today's factories.

8. Noah's Shattering Act of Violence

Any objection to calling Noah's act of killing the animals a "shattering act of violence," then, trades primarily on modern disregard for nonhuman animals. For to speak of this as a shattering act of violence is perfectly consistent even with the perspective of those ancient Hebrews who affirmed the practice of animal sacrifice. Again, it is precisely the shattering violence of the act that makes it significant enough to function as a real sacrifice. Therefore, from the ancient Israelites' perspective, and presumably from the perspective of any society that offers sincere animal sacrifices, it most certainly is a shattering act of violence. So the question is not whether or not Noah's act constitutes a shattering act of violence; it indubitably does. The question is whether or not the Flood narrative is one of those narratives that must be rejected insofar as it confusedly affirms that the deity is pleased and placated by such acts of violence.

In an earlier narrative context, the account of Noah's ritual act of sacrifice quite probably did affirm ritual sacrifice and thus would require criticism. But, as I will argue presently, there are very good reasons to affirm that our received Genesis version of Noah's sacrifice should not be subject to such criticism because in a subtle but definite way, the earlier version of the narrative was transformed and made into an integral part of the Hebrew Scripture's prophetic critique of both sacrifice and tit-for-tat understandings of covenantal relationship with the divine.

I will argue in the next section that the Genesis version of the Flood is wholly consistent with the critique of sacrifice found in Micah and Isaiah, and I will argue that the Flood narrative in Genesis decisively rejects bloody tit-for-tat covenantal thinking and proclaims in its stead the nonreciprocal, absolute, loving, and even gracious character of the divine. I would suggest that it is this mature affirmation of humans' covenantal relationship with the divine, an affirmation at the very heart of the primeval history, that, at a relatively late date in the composition, compiling, and editing of Hebrew Scripture, earned the primeval history its pivotal place at the very beginning of Genesis.

In the preceding chapters I worked to justify a legitimate way of critically opening ourselves to the testimony of spiritual classics and to disarm materialistic tendencies. In this chapter I have attempted at least to begin to disarm an anthropocentrism that has long prejudiced interpretations of the Flood narrative. Now, in the larger context of my overall attempt to begin to articulate how we might orient ourselves spiritually, with eyes wide open to all the suffering and injustice suffusing reality, I will explore the Flood and Creation narratives for insight. I will begin with the Flood narrative, particularly with the dramatic conclusion of the Flood narrative proper, namely, with the so-called Noahic covenant, the "never again" covenant that God famously seals with a rainbow.

CHAPTER FIVE

Aftermath

The Birth of the God of Grace

1. The So-called Noahic Covenant

The Flood narrative proper concludes with the so-called Noahic covenant. I say "so-called" Noahic covenant because this common title (which one can find inserted into many translations as a section heading) reflects the anthropocentrism of modern culture and profoundly misrepresents the character of the covenant. It is important to note that there was no deliberate plot to exclude all nonhuman creatures in the misnaming of this covenant. Modern commentators were not even conscious of the exclusion. Rather, they were so conditioned by modernity's anthropocentrism that they simply did not notice the blatant and repeated inclusion of every creature and even the earth itself in the covenant. Let me cite this famous text in full, using italics to highlight the portions that the standard modern title "Noahic covenant" elides. Note who is included in the covenantal relationship in the sections in italics.

> Then God said to Noah and to his sons with him, "As for me, I am establishing my covenant with you and your descendants after you, *and with every living creature that is with you, the birds, the domestic animals, and every animal of the earth with you, as many as came out of the ark.* I establish my covenant with you, that never again shall *all flesh* be cut off by the waters of a flood, and never again shall there be a flood to destroy *the earth.*" God said, "This is the sign of the covenant that I make between

me and you *and every living creature that is with you,* for all future generations: I have set my bow in the clouds, and it shall be a sign of the covenant between me and *the earth.* When I bring clouds over the earth and the bow is seen in the clouds, I will remember my covenant that is between me and you *and every living creature of all flesh;* and the waters shall never again become a flood to destroy *all flesh.* When the bow is in the clouds, I will see it and remember the everlasting covenant between God *and every living creature of all flesh that is on the earth.*" God said to Noah, "This is the sign of the covenant that I have established between me *and all flesh that is on the earth.*" (Gen. 9:8-17)

Once we remove the anthropocentric lenses, it is stunningly obvious that calling this the "Noahic covenant" radically misrepresents the scope of divine concern expressed by the narrative. God is portrayed speaking directly to Noah, but what God tells Noah — repeatedly — is that the bow is a sign of an "everlasting covenant between God and *every living creature of all flesh that is on the earth.*" Insofar as the misreading of this text as a covenant exclusively between God and humans facilitates theological understandings that portray nonhuman creatures and the rest of creation as outside the scope of divine concern, it facilitates real violence in the world.

Significantly, in marked contrast to the tit-for-tat economy set up by the conditional character of covenants that require obedience — and, in bloodier variants, sacrificial offerings — the rainbow covenant is clearly unilateral in character.[1] Nowhere does one find a list of demands that humans or other creatures must meet in order to fulfill their side of the deal. Only God speaks, and only God makes a commitment. And that commitment is a unilateral and unconditional rejection of the violence and devastation of the Flood even when one takes account of all the wickedness that covered the face of the earth: Never again. Nowhere in the rainbow covenant does one find a demand for sacrifices. This most certainly is not a tit-for-tat covenant, let alone a bloody one.

1. In recent years it has become more common to hear this called the "earth covenant." That is appropriate and much better than "Noahic covenant." But I will refer to it as the "rainbow covenant" because the experience of rainbows, that is, of delight, beauty, joy, and peace, which often appear amidst stormy weather, nicely captures the spirit of the passage.

The rainbow covenant concludes the Flood narrative proper within the larger narrative arc of the primeval history of Genesis 1–11. Clearly, it stands at utter odds with both aspects of Noah's shattering act of violence. That is, by the time one reaches the rainbow covenant, it is clear that the Flood narrative as a whole has rejected both Noah's shattering act of violence and Noah's attempt to initiate a tit-for-tat covenantal relationship with God. Let me now explore in more detail the character and significance of this stunning development.

2. From the Ultimacy of Justice to the Ultimacy of Grace

Recall that first and foremost the ancients were survivors and the children of survivors who were confronted with the reality of a devastating flood. And remember that the generations that carried forward the Flood narratives in diverse oral and eventually written traditions faced a multitude of devastating tragedies that were similar in kind (from smaller floods to drought and famine, to death from snakebite, to death in childbirth, to disease or infection). In their struggle to make sense of such tragedies, they assumed that the world was meaningful and that everything that happened on earth was caught up in some purpose. And so they interpreted natural events on analogy with their interpretation of human actions. That is, they asked even with regard to natural events, "Why has this happened? What intention was served?" They assumed that behind natural forces (rain, wind, disease, and death) there was a humanlike agent (or agents) acting with considered motives.

This assumption is utterly common not only among ancient peoples but even today among people confronted with natural disasters. Moreover, one common response to disasters small and large is to interpret them as the result of divine judgment and to accept the judgment without protest, that is, to view it as well deserved. This is congruent with the devastating way in which moral people can find themselves unable to affirm existence in the face of all the suffering and injustice suffusing reality. To the degree that a people is sensitive to all creatures, the surpassing, damning reality of the abyss is overwhelming. And in that context, when something awful happens, it is not surprising for a people to conclude that somehow the suffering has been deserved. Nor, as a corollary, is the idea that survivors must have been relatively pleasing to the gods. So we should not be surprised that in other versions of the Noah Flood narrative (i.e., extrabiblical versions different from the two versions that have been edited into the single narrative we now find in Genesis), Noah's survival was attributed to his righteousness and the horrifying deaths of everyone else were attributed to their wickedness.[2]

But modern Westerners no longer consider every natural event to be the direct result of some divine intention. And in accord with my spirituality/science distinction, I affirm natural interpretations of natural events. For instance, the Indian Ocean tsunami of 2004, the Haiti earthquake of 2009, and the Japan tsunami of 2011 were all caused not by any agent but by the movements of tectonic plates. Likewise, there is no reason to doubt that whatever caused the massive flood that stood behind the diverse Ancient Near Eastern flood narratives, it was also a natural event (e.g., tsunami, thousand-year flood, collapse of an ice dam, and so forth). Moreover — now thinking morally — I do not think that the awful death of all the families of all the creatures on earth aside from Noah's is a good, loving, or even just response to human sin. In short, on both scientific and theological grounds, I reject the idea that God sent a devastating flood that killed all the families of all creatures on earth because of human wickedness.

This may sound like a rejection of the Flood narrative in Genesis. In fact, it is not. On the contrary, while it is indeed a rejection of the science of the account (i.e., that God sent the Flood), and while it is a rejection of earlier versions of the Flood narrative that see the Flood as the justifiable response of a righteous god, my rejection of the idea that God sent a devastating Flood is utterly consistent with the spirituality of the extant Genesis version of the narrative, and particularly with its understanding of God. For, together with the Genesis narrative, I reject the sending of the Flood as an action consistent with my own or, I am arguing, with Judaism's or Christianity's most profound convictions about the ultimate character of the divine.[3]

2. See Wayne Baxter, "Noahic Traditions and the *Book of Noah*," *Journal for the Study of the Pseudepigrapha* 15, no. 3 (2006): 179-94.

3. Notably, many people who are hostile to religion make a point of rejecting the God of Genesis precisely because they are so morally offended by any God who would kill almost every male, female, and juvenile of every species on earth because of the

Note well that in the course of the narrative, the rainbow covenant signals a remarkable change *in God*. The God who had just responded to the wickedness filling the earth with a devastating flood now, in the immediate aftermath of the Flood, vows unilaterally and unconditionally with regard to similar or even worse circumstances: *Never again*. One might recall in this regard the judgments and reactions of the gods in the flood story of the Gilgamesh Epic, namely, the judgment and action of Enlil ("Kill them all with a deluge!"); of Ea ("It is wrong to kill them all; I will instruct Uta-napisti in order to save the seeds of all life"); and of Belet-ili ("I was wrong to agree to the deluge, and I create this lapis lazuli necklace so that I will never forget"). Belet-ili's reaction was eventually the reaction of all the gods. All of these judgments and reactions, which are attributed to three gods in Gilgamesh, appear again in Genesis, this time attributed in sequence to Israel's one God.

With this stunning transition in God, placed at the very beginning of Hebrew Scripture, we encounter an unambiguous proclamation of a God of grace, of a God who steps beyond any tit-for-tat economy of exchange, of a God who will no longer return evil for evil, of a God who rejects violence as a way to achieve the peaceable creation. This is that same God, of course, who is disgusted with the blood and violence of sacrifice, who is pleased by people when they do justice, love kindness, and walk humbly on the face of the earth, and who expects love and pursuit of justice to flow forth in response to a gift received. In short, in an astonishing development, the final redactors of the primeval history offer up the Flood narrative as, above all, the story of the birth of the God of grace.

Notably, this means that, in the end, the Genesis version of the Flood narrative is wholly resonant with moral rejection of the idea that God should send a devastating flood that would kill almost all families on earth in response to human wickedness. People often criticize the Jewish and Christian faiths by invoking the injustice of the Flood and by pointing to the unacceptable horror of the drowning of all those other, unnamed families of all kinds. The good spiritual sensitivities that provoke this critique are wholly

---

sin of even a multitude of humans. I am not only agreeing with their moral offense; I am suggesting that the narrative itself clearly agrees with their evaluation. If this is the case, the narrative deserves a second, more careful look on the part of those who reject it on said grounds.

resonant with the spiritual sensitivities of those who composed the extant Genesis version of the Flood narrative, for by the close of the narrative, God is portrayed reaching precisely the same conclusion about the horrors of the Flood. God is transformed in the wake of the horrors of the Flood. And now God says unilaterally, unconditionally, and repeatedly, "Never again!"

The redactors who give us the Flood narrative in Genesis thus agree that the God who would bring such a flood is not the God they know, for the God they know is a God not only of justice, but also and ultimately a God of love and grace. And so they resolve the dissonance between the well-established, bloody, tit-for-tat traditions that they have received and their convictions about the character of divinity by asserting that the experience of the Flood results in a change in God and in a change in the way God relates to the world. Again, in their hands the Flood narrative is primarily about a stunning change in God: it narrates the birth of a God who is now above all a God of grace.

By the time various ancient Israelite flood traditions are combined by the Genesis redactors, those traditions — including, prominently, bloody tit-for-tat traditions — are well established and powerful within the community. So the Genesis redactors who give us the final form of the primeval narrative make a daring move when they reject interpretive traditions that affirm the flood as justified divine judgment and instead support and develop an interpretive tradition that sees the Flood as an unjustifiable horror, that turns the Flood narrative into a proclamation of grace above all.

Today we are far enough removed from the authority of these earlier traditions to criticize them in a more straightforward fashion. Namely, I do not need to assert a change in the character of the divine, a change in the divine from wrathfulness to grace, a change from a God who bizarrely seeks to achieve justice and peace through unimaginable global violence (i.e., the Flood) to a God of love and grace. Instead, I can interpret this narrative as a marker of a human conceptual transition that takes a quantum leap beyond bloody tit-for-tat understandings of a relationship with divinity, which takes a quantum step beyond any economy of justice, which takes the quantum step to proclamation that ultimately divinity is characterized by gracious love. Thus does this conceptual, spiritual leap name a conviction that the justice of divine righteousness is, ultimately, secondary to divine love and grace.[4] If *grace, not justice,* marks the primordial and ultimate character of reality, then perhaps — even with eyes wide open to all the suffering and injustice suffusing reality — *grace, not damnation,* is primordial and ultimate.

3. What Transforms God?

What, according to the narrative, wrought this profound change in God? The most obvious proximate event is clearly the traumatic experience of the horrors of the Flood itself. Those horrors are certainly in play, for it is only in their wake that the immediate precipitating event, which in and of itself pales in comparison with the obliteration of virtually all life on earth, attains sufficient gravity to inspire transformation in God. Before proceeding directly to the immediate precipitating event that wrought this profound change in God, however, it will be helpful to answer two preliminary questions. First, according to the narrative, why did God unleash the Flood? And second, according to the narrative, what did God hope to accomplish?

The opening parts of the Flood narrative in Genesis highlight the wickedness of humanity on the face of the earth and emphasize that it was because of the wickedness of humans that God brought the great Flood. At the

---

4. The redactors/authors of the primeval narrative represent only one voice in an ongoing debate about the character of the deity that continued in ancient Jewish thought and beyond. Indeed, today many Christians still believe that God needed the death of Jesus Christ on the cross as necessary and just recompense for human wickedness (that is to say, bloody tit-for-tat covenant interpretations are still out there). Other Christians see the heart of atonement theory not in satisfaction of a demand for blood and death that is realized in the murder of Jesus on the cross, but in the vulnerable way of love visible in divinity that is seen as God in the flesh, who proclaims *for* the weak and oppressed and *against* the rich and oppressive, who speaks for righteousness in the face of injustice, for love in the face of selfishness, and who remains true to the way of peace, love, and righteousness, even to death on a cross. From this latter perspective, the Christ event (manger, proclamation, cross) is the signal manifestation in extremis of divinity's nonviolent, noncoercive, gracious character, a love realized most dramatically not in the killing of almost every creature on earth but in a life that remains courageously committed to justice, righteousness, grace, and speaking the truth about injustice to an oppressive power all the way to a brutal and unjust death. The Genesis Flood narrative and this latter understanding of the Christ event, then, offer parallel spiritual testimony.

same time, the narrative relates the righteousness of Noah and emphasizes that it is because of his righteousness that Noah and his family were saved. Given this clear thematic trajectory, one would expect that what is evidently God's plan would succeed, namely, that the Flood would finish off the disastrous trajectory initiated by the rebellion of Adam and Eve, and that then, beginning from righteous Noah and his family, as well as from two of each kind of every other creature on earth, humans and all other creatures would go forth from the ark and multiply upon a newly righteous earth.

It takes only a moment's reflection on the overall context of the primeval history (i.e., Gen. 1–11) to realize that this interpretation of God's unleashing of the Flood as a wise and effective act is set up early in the narrative only to be decisively rejected. The primeval history as a whole ends with the Tower of Babel narrative. At the heart of that narrative (which, let me emphasize, comes close on the heels of the Flood narrative) one immediately finds once again a people who have forgotten God, a people who are obsessed with making a name for themselves through material and military strength (i.e., by building a city with a mighty tower), a people so rebellious that once again God, as in the Flood narrative, acts forcefully and decisively, but this time not lethally — that is, by scattering people into different language groups.

Notably, the transition from the primeval narrative (i.e., Gen. 1–11) to the balance of Genesis (Genesis 12–50) comes with the transition from the narrative of the tower builders of Babel to the narrative of the call of Abram (later renamed Abraham). In stark contrast to the city/tower builders of Babel, who were intent on "making a name for themselves," the call of the Abram narrative makes it clear that it is God who will make Abram's name great, for the sake of all the families of the earth (including all those families that came out of the ark):

> I will make of you a great nation, and I will bless you, and make your name great, so that you will be a blessing. I will bless those who bless you, and the one who curses you I will curse; and in you all the families of the earth shall be blessed. (Gen. 12:2-3)

With this text I am pushing beyond the boundaries of our study. But by this time it is clear that, far from signaling any success in wiping the wicked from the face of the earth while preserving the righteous, the primeval narrative in the wake of the Flood very quickly takes us back to an earth full of people who have forgotten God and who are bent on making a name for themselves via material power. Even a brief reflection on the overall narrative arc of the primeval history, then, makes it clear that the narrative itself decisively precludes any interpretation of God's unleashing of the Flood as a wise and effective way to ensure that once again the face of the earth will be covered with righteousness, for in the immediate wake of the Flood the earth is again full of people who have forgotten God.

The rejection of the idea of the Flood as a wise and effective way to return righteousness to the earth, however, comes even before the Tower of Babel narrative. In the passage that immediately follows the rainbow covenant (Gen. 9:18-29) we are told one final story about Noah. He plants a vineyard, makes wine, gets drunk, lies "uncovered" in his tent (a euphemism for being found in some kind of sexually compromising position), and is seen in that state by one of his three sons, Ham. When Noah sobers up, he is so offended by Ham's witnessing his "nakedness" (that euphemism again) that he curses his son, declaring that the "lowest of the slaves shall he be to his brothers." Noah then blesses his other two sons, Shem and Japheth, and concludes with his only recorded words in Genesis with this: "[A]nd let Canaan [i.e., the purported territory of Ham's descendants] be [Shem's and Japheth's] slave."[5] Then the text notes briefly that Noah, who was then 600 years old, lived another 350 years and died.[6]

5. I should note explicitly that this story of the curse of Ham is precisely the text used so despicably by some nineteenth-century Christians to justify the enslavement of Africans (the idea being that the African peoples are the descendants of Ham). Unfortunately, such oppressive use of this text is not anachronistic, for in its ancient context this text, which is certainly older than our received narrative, almost certainly functioned to justify the Israelites' violent takeover of the land of Canaan. That is, there were profound and deep cultural and political reasons to preserve this text and to affirm the correctness of the curse upon Ham and his descendants, for it served to justify a political status quo that was the result of oppressive violence. To the degree that this text was and/or is used to justify the oppression and even enslavement of people (and it is not clear what other significance it might have, other than to reinforce the point that Noah, too, is imperfect), we should reject it.

6. One obstacle to affirming any ambiguity about Noah may be related to a modern Western tendency to be intolerant of ambiguity in its heroes. Let me emphasize by

This text's comment on Noah is not as wholly negative as it first appears. In the first place, the portrayal of Noah as cultivating the land finds him positively living out the stewardship call issued to Adam and Eve. Second, the attribution of incredible age was a standard narrative device meant to signal God's favor, insofar as God has blessed one with a long life. This is certainly consistent with the Flood narrative's regard for Noah as a righteous man who was pleasing to God. This regard, we should remember, was most likely a prominent aspect of the received tit-for-tat traditions with which the Genesis primeval narrative redactors are dealing.

Nonetheless, there is no denying the negative portrayal of Noah's being drunk, passed out, and caught in a sexually compromising position so significant that it leads not only to lifelong alienation from one of his three sons but to a curse that Ham and all his heirs might be forever enslaved by his brothers and their heirs. Notably, Noah's tit-for-tat response contrasts markedly with the gracious response of God in the "rainbow covenant." And in terms of the narrative arc of the primeval history, the imperfections of Noah and the birth of conflict between him and one of his sons, and the birth of slavery among his sons and their progeny, fit with a trajectory of a new spread of conflict and ungodliness over the face of the earth in the wake of the Flood (i.e., this is essentially a second "Fall" narrative). Therefore, the primeval history goes on to end not with a new and righteous world resulting from the Flood and God's preservation of Noah and his family and the animals, but with the story of the Tower of Babel.

But it is not primarily the overall thematic arc of the primeval narrative that rejects any valorization of the Flood as wise and effective and rejects any idolizing of Noah as perfectly righteous. The divine realization that it is futile to depend on the righteousness of Noah comes before the story of the people of Babel, and even before the narrative of Noah's drunkenness, sexual compromise, family alienation, and instantiation of slavery. The pivotal turn lies at the very heart of the Flood narrative in

---

contrast that realistic acknowledgment of the ambiguous character of even heroes of faith is patent among the ancient Israelites. To cite only the most famous example, think of David (the great king of the Davidic covenant), whose famous psalms of confession are partly related to his infamous lust for Bathsheba, a lust so profound that he ordered that her husband, Uriah, one of his own soldiers, be placed in the front lines and then quickly abandoned in a sudden retreat so that he would be slaughtered (2 Sam. 11).

Genesis. In the immediate wake of the unspeakable horrors of the Flood, it is Noah's shattering act of violence, the slaughter of animals for sacrifice, which inspires the stunning and stupendous transformation in God. The precipitating event, an event that on superficial measure is of small scale, an event whose true significance is manifest in the hyperrefined moral sensitivity stimulated by the horrors of the Flood, is Noah's shattering act of violence, an act that in the wake of the unspeakable horror and devastation of the Flood is absurd and awful and horrifying enough to shake God to new depths of realization and commitment.

Up until the moment of Noah's sacrifice, the narrative encourages us to see justice done, to see the wicked vanquished and the righteous preserved. The earth is full of wickedness. The righteous Noah and the seed of the peaceable creation are preserved on the ark. The waters recede. The ark is opened. Noah and his family emerge. In a sweet touch, *families* of creatures of every kind emerge peaceably from the ark. All are saved — all are safe. God issues an all-inclusive blessing, proclaiming that creatures of every kind are to be fruitful and are to multiply. Though the horror of the Flood is proximate, we are encouraged to see justice done and to anticipate a new beginning, a new day when righteousness will cover the face of the earth.

But just as a new light is apparently dawning, just as dry land suitable for life again appears, the ark is opened, the seed of the new peaceable creation begins to go forth — just then the narrative abruptly shifts to the shattering act of violence: Noah's decision to attempt to dictate tit-for-tat terms of relationship to God with a bloody offering. And when God smells the sweet odor (bringing to mind the sickly sweet odor of burnt flesh), when God smells the twofold offense of Noah — the tit-for-tat initiative and also the offense of the bloody slaughter — two transformative realizations dawn on God.[7] First of all, humans will never be righteous. Every

---

7. A common and misleading translation speaks of God smelling the "pleasing odor" of the sacrifice. "Pleasing" is a possible translation but carries a sense of affirmation that the Hebrew does not require. Given the contextual rejection of the bloody tit-for-tat ritual sacrifice, it is better to speak of the "sweet odor" of the burnt offering, and to interpret that in line with the sickly scent brought to mind when the reference is to the flesh of humans burnt in accidents or in war, where one often hears reference to the "sickly sweet smell of burnt flesh." There are contexts in the Hebrew Scriptures

human, even Noah, is wicked. There is no hope to be had in a new beginning, for "the inclination of the human heart is evil from youth" (Gen. 8:21). That is the first, pivotal, awful realization.

But the vindictive, destructive energy is spent. Moreover, in the wake of hyperrefined sensitivity to suffering stimulated by the horrors of the Flood, Noah's bloody slaughter is the decisive slap in the face of the deity. The second pivotal and awesome realization dawns: violence does not bring redemption; violence provides no recompense for evil; violence yields no spiritual renewal or transformation. Even if in some circumstances it may represent the least bad alternative, violence is always itself evil. Noah's shattering act of violence, his slaughter of those beloved creatures, was evil. The Flood was evil. That is the second pivotal and awesome realization: violence does not redeem; violence provides no recompense for evil; and violence yields no spiritual renewal or transformation.

This second realization is stimulated above all by an infinitely heightened sensitivity to the well-being of every creature. It is a sensitivity born of the haunting cries of every one of those screaming, weeping, drowning creatures. And insofar as it is a realization wholly stimulated by love, insofar as it is wholly a response to that love, a having been seized by an infinite, impassioned, all-consuming desire in the wake of the horror, an all-consuming desire for the good and flourishing and joy of every other, it is a realization that itself steps wholly beyond every tit-for-tat economy, a realization that brings upon oneself, that brings upon God (who, like Enli, is responsible for the Flood and its horrors), *no condemnation,* not even in the moment when the reality of the evil that has been committed is wholly brought home.[8]

What remains is impossible, enduring, all-consuming, gracious love

---

where "pleasing odor" may be not only grammatically permissible but the contextually appropriate translation. This is not one of those contexts.

8. I would suggest that this is the transition that scholars are marking in technical language when they speak of the triumph of grace (e.g., Karl Barth) or of the way in which the gift displaces every economy (e.g., Jean-Luc Marion), or of a form of theology that is done without theodicy because the challenge to which theodicy constitutes a reply simply never arises (e.g., Emmanuel Levinas). In technical phenomenological rhetoric, along the lines of Levinas and Marion, one might roughly call this the narrative of the birth of the gift.

— toward others, toward ourselves. Not even Noah proves righteous, but the waters of chaos are not unleashed again, this time to finish the job. For the realization that no human will ever be righteous, that a relationship predicated on righteousness can never be realized, that first realization dawns with the second, even more awesome realization, the realization that transforms the divine, the realization wherein the God of ultimate grace, the God of the rainbow covenant, is born. Noah's shattering act of violence, precisely as evil and offensive, precisely as it *seizes God as evil and offensive,* precisely as it is an aggressive tit-for-tat economy, precisely as infinite bloody violation, precisely as it replicates the bloody, beyond tit-for-tat evil that was the unleashing of the Flood — is the act that finally provokes an astounding change in the very heart of God and gives birth to a God whose own be-ing and relationship to creation is now first and last a realization and manifestation of gracious love.

God smells the (sickly) sweet smell of the sacrifice, and God says "in his heart, 'I will never again curse the ground because of humankind, for the inclination of the human heart is evil from youth'" (Gen. 8:21). And God names this evil, this truth, without a thought toward any tit-for-tat economy of justice and without being overcome by guilt. The proclamation that grace is ultimate, that God is ultimately a God of grace, the proclamation amplified and made fully explicit in the rainbow covenant, is already fully present in the spiritual dynamics of this "never again" in God's "heart."

4. God's Realistic Blessing

The Flood narrative, continuing in parallel to the Creation narrative, moves to recount God's blessing of humans.[9] In contrast to the blessing of the first humans in the seven-days-of-Creation narrative, where God declares all that has been created to be "good," day after day, where sin has yet to be introduced into the picture, God blesses these humans, proclaim-

---

9. Where I speak of God's blessing of humans, the text actually names a blessing of "Noah and his sons." The exclusion of women reflects a problematic patriarchal heritage that devalues women and on occasion afflicts Hebrew Scripture.

ing the divine intent that they "be fruitful and multiply, and fill the earth," despite the fact that they are "evil from youth" (Gen. 9:1; the blessing is repeated in v. 7). The true depth of this blessing is clearer in this context than it is in the pre-Fall, perfectly good context of the seven-days-of-Creation narrative, for in this context it is clear that love endures despite the fact that "the human heart is evil from youth." Christians have traditionally marked this depth and endurance of love by speaking of "grace," which does not name anything other than love, but specifies that true love (in the sense of the Hebrew *hesed*, or the Greek agape, or the English "altruism") is a love that prevails even in the face of evil.

However, as will become even clearer when I explicitly examine the seven-days narrative, even if the reality of sin in a fallen creation does not defeat God's love, it definitively qualifies God's wholly realistic assessment of humanity and the Creation. As I will point out in the next chapter, the seven-days-of-Creation narrative paints the picture of a peaceable creation where none kill to live and all live in perfect harmony, a peaceable world in which we humans, along with every other kind of creature, eat only seeds and fruits. As we will see, it is this vegan, peaceable creation that God proclaims to be "very good" in the seven-days narrative.

Now, however, in the wake of Noah's shattering act of violence and in the wake of the realization that "the inclination of the human heart is evil from youth," we are told that every other animal has been delivered into our hands, and we will also have them for food. Not surprisingly, in marked contrast to the peaceable creation visible in the ark and in the seven-days-of-Creation narrative, now it is specified that the "fear and dread" of humans will rest on every creature of the earth. The narrative still insists on ritual respect for every creature's life, dictating that we are not to eat flesh that still contains "its life, that is, its blood." And the narrative dictates special respect for humans, since they are made in the image of God, specifying that God will require capital punishment for every animal (including humans) that takes a human life.

Obviously, far from being a picture of God's ideal world, what we hear here is a description of the real world, a world full of fear, dread, killing, eating of meat, murder, and capital punishment. This is not the picture of a world that God would declare "very good." This is the picture of a world where humans, whose hearts are inclined to evil from youth, have been fruitful and have multiplied. The picture is hyperrealistic and stunning. It is the world we know, a world where suffering, killing, and wickedness cover the face of the earth.

In this context there is a very notable and not at all surprising distinction between the blessing of humans in the seven-days-of-Creation narrative and the Flood narrative, where a *nearly* identical blessing is repeated. In the seven-days-of-Creation narrative the famous blessing reads: "God blessed them, and God said to them, 'Be fruitful and multiply, and fill the earth and subdue it; and have dominion over . . . every living thing that moves upon the earth'" (Gen. 1:28). An almost exact parallel to this "be fruitful and multiply" blessing occurs twice in the context of the Flood narrative (Gen. 9:1 and 9:7). The two occurrences of the blessing in the Flood narrative serve as a frame for the very realistic description of the world I just mentioned, in which humans, whose hearts are inclined toward evil, have flourished (Gen. 9:2-6). And on both occasions the blessing is decisively truncated: "Be fruitful and multiply, and fill the earth" (9:1), and "be fruitful and multiply, abound on the earth and multiply in it" (9:7). The famous final phrases of the blessing as it is found in the seven-days-of-Creation narrative, the "subdue" and "have dominion" phrases, are markedly and wholly absent.

The absence of the "subdue" and "have dominion" commands is notable but not surprising, because it reflects an entirely reasonable and realistic response to the recognition that "the inclination of the human heart is evil from youth." Given this realism about humans, God is quite reasonably portrayed as *not* giving divine sanction to human rule and dominion. I can only detail the full significance of this in light of our reading of the seven-days-of-Creation narrative. Already here, however, I can note the realistic and sobering contrast between the blessing in the seven-days-of-Creation and the Flood narratives. Let me hasten to say, however, that realism in this context is not meant to induce condemnation or despair. The focus of this narrative is most definitely not on the wickedness of humanity but on the grace of God, on the primordial and ultimate reign of grace, on grace in a context that remains brutal.

The blessing that frames this awful and realistic description of the real world is truncated, but the divine blessing endures. In this spirit, unfolding the spiritual dynamics so tightly wound up in "I will never again curse the ground because of humankind, for the inclination of the human heart is evil from youth," the narrative moves rapidly from this moving and realistic depiction of creation to the rainbow covenant. Indeed, in the wake of this realistic picture of an earth full of wickedness, our contrasting wonder and joy over the rainbow covenant is accentuated. For insofar as this covenant comes in the immediate wake of this description of a wicked, fallen world — a violent world full of fear, dread, killing, eating of meat, murder, and capital punishment — the divine "never again" unmistakably signifies that we are dealing not only with a God of justice but ultimately and foremost with a God of grace.

In summary, with full knowledge of the irremediable depths of human wickedness, the final Genesis redactors proclaim that this newly born God of grace, this God fully aware of the enduring wickedness of the human heart and fully aware of all the enduring injustice, strife, and suffering that fill the earth — this God still enters unconditionally and unilaterally into covenantal relationships with all of us, with every creature, even with the earth herself. Here there is utter rejection of bloody, tit-for-tat covenantal understanding, and in its place there is an affirmation, eyes wide open to all the injustice and suffering that suffuse reality, of the primordial and ultimate reality of gracious love.

Inspired by the primordial and ultimate reality of gracious love, the authors/redactors of the primeval history vision seek to testify to it and to inspire it in others, to awaken us to having been seized by love for every creature, to give us a vision of what God's perfectly perfect peaceable creation would look like. Herein, I suggest, lies the inspiration and goal of the seven-days-of-Creation narrative.

CHAPTER SIX

The Seven Days of Creation

1. Creation Spirituality and the Two Creation Narratives

The seven-days-of-Creation narrative is probably best known in the modern West as it is related to the controversies over evolution, creation science, and intelligent-design theory. The creationists and intelligent-design theorists are correct to think that there is something about a predominant stream of modern Western thought that poses a clear and illegitimate threat to classic spiritual belief (a threat to all faith and moral-realist traditions). I have identified that stream of modern thought as materialism (it is also called scientism, physicalism, or naturalism). Insofar as creation science and intelligent-design theory are attempts to argue for the existence of God with scientific or philosophical arguments, however, creationists are themselves operating within naturalistic parameters, just like those among their opponents who claim that modern science has disproven the possibility of spiritual reality in the classic sense.[1] As a result, as I have argued, creationists and their opponents all end up providing us with both confused science and confused spirituality.

Apart from the debates over evolution and creation science, the two

---

1. Arguably, what one gets when one takes a positivist mentality and applies it to theology is fundamentalism. That is, in philosophical terms one could describe fundamentalism as the spawn of twentieth-century philosophical/logical positivism blossoming within the sphere of the world's religions.

Creation narratives in Genesis (i.e., the seven-days-of-Creation and the Adam-and-Eve narratives) have been best known for the past few decades with respect to their significance for environmental concerns. When it comes to environmental concerns, the two narratives have typically been pitted against one another. In recent decades, the Adam-and-Eve narrative has been used when theologians want to affirm the value of nature and to emphasize that humans should be good stewards of the earth. There is good reason for this: the narrative portrays Adam and Eve as caretakers of God's garden and emphasizes the link between humans and the earth. Adam, for instance, is created "from dust." In Hebrew, it is "Adam from *Adamah*" (meaning "earth"). So "Adam from *Adamah*" might best be translated "human from humus." (God creates Eve, of course, out of the side of Adam, so she is equally connected to the earth.) Furthermore, God places Adam in the garden in order to till and care for it. I will not reflect in any detail on this subtle narrative, but already two of its most basic points are apparent: humans are intimately related to the earth, and they are expressly created to be good stewards of the earth, caretakers of God's garden.

Far more influentially, however, the seven-days-of-Creation narrative has long been interpreted quite to the contrary. Our distinction from and superiority to the rest of creation has been emphasized. For millennia — and especially in the modern West — the seven-days narrative has been celebrated for depicting a seemingly clear hierarchy within creation, with humans at the top. Indeed, from its majestic opening, "In the beginning God created the heavens and the earth," to the famous passage that portrays our creation in the image of God, Christians have long found it easy to read in the first Creation narrative a wondrous celebration and glorification of humanity: humans are created in the image of God, are blessed, are told to be fruitful and to multiply, to subdue the earth, and to have dominion over all creatures. In accordance with this seemingly straightforward picture, many Christians through the centuries have argued that we alone within creation are significant, that "natural resources" and "animals" were created as gifts for our use and pleasure, and that stewardship is a reference only to our responsibility to preserve resources for our grandchildren and great-grandchildren.

Modern Western thought has typically excluded nonhuman animals from the moral sphere. And within such an anthropocentric conceptual context, it has seemed obvious that the seven-days narrative glorifies humanity and accords all other creatures only instrumental value. It is not surprising, then, that those who were caught in the conceptual grip of anthropocentrism quite naturally understood the seven-days narrative to be focused on the divine blessing and celebration of humanity.

In this spirit, for instance, in 1994 the textual commentary in the New Oxford Revised Standard Version of the Bible, generally considered to be among the most progressive of twentieth-century translation projects, introduced the seven-days narrative with this comment: "Out of original chaos God created an orderly world, assigning a preeminent place to human beings."[2] This comment glorifies humanity while diminishing the independent worth of the rest of creation and simply ignoring all other creatures.

Such confused interpretation is not surprising when one takes into account the anthropocentrism that has long plagued Western thought and that has been, as I have explained, amplified in the modern West to the nth degree. Notably, this means one should critique such confusion with a generous spirit. For while anthropocentric misreadings of the seven-days narrative are indeed self-serving and confused, it remains true that, no matter how misguided, the misreadings have not been overtly willful or calculated. Within the anthropocentric modern Western conceptual context they have simply seemed obvious.

Unfortunately, anthropocentric readings of the seven-days-of-Creation narrative have not only seemed obvious but, because of the profound influence of Christianity in the West, they have been profoundly influential. Thus it is not surprising that in 1967, in the journal *Science*, Lynn White published a famous and widely anthologized essay entitled "The Historical Roots of Our Ecologic Crisis," in which he attacked Christianity for what he called the "huge burden of guilt" it bore for our ecological crisis.[3] White apparently saw the Genesis Creation narratives as irredeemable, but he thought that Christians had other spiritual resources, and he

---

2. *The New Oxford Annotated Bible*, ed. Bruce Metzger and Roland Murphy (New York: Oxford University Press, 1994), p. 2. A slightly different version of this sentence was in the 1977 edition of this Bible. A wholly new set of notes was introduced in the 2001 edition, and this line no longer appears.

3. Lynn White, "The Historical Roots of Our Ecologic Crisis," *Science* 155, no. 3767 (March 10, 1967): 1206.

called on Christians to reform themselves, harking back to the spiritual wisdom of the likes of Saint Francis of Assisi, the patron saint of animals.[4]

The first thing Christians (like myself) should do, when confronted with White's accusation, is confess. For Christianity has indeed been appropriated to justify the abuse and exploitation of creation. And perhaps no passage of Scripture has been appropriated more powerfully to justify abuse of creation than the seven-days-of-Creation narrative. But while White's condemnation of the predominant modern Western Christian understanding of humanity's relationship to creation is justified, it turns out that anthropocentric interpretation of the seven-days narrative is wholly confused.

Just as anthropocentric interpretation seemed obvious within an anthropocentric context, in the light of awakening to love for all creatures, it becomes clear that the seven-days-of-Creation narrative calls us to a profound creation spirituality. Indeed, the creation spirituality of the seven-days narrative is even more unambiguous and profound than that of the Adam-and-Eve narrative. For while the Adam-and-Eve narrative calls us to be stewards of creation, the seven-days narrative calls us not merely to stewardship of all creation but to a love for all creatures. As will become clear, the creation spirituality for which Saint Francis of Assisi is celebrated, the Christian spirituality Lynn White rightly praised, is in fact the spirituality of the seven-days-of-Creation narrative.

In stark opposition to the standard modern reading, then, I will make clear how the seven-days narrative testifies to a profoundly gracious spirituality vis-à-vis all creatures and all creation, a testimony that is even more poignant, powerful, demanding, and spiritually invigorating than the Adam-and-Eve narrative's call to stewardship. It will become clear that it is utterly confused to think that the seven-days narrative glorifies humanity and values other creatures and the rest of creation as gifts given for human use and enjoyment. Contrary to the predominant modern understanding, I will argue that the seven-days narrative is inspired by and seeks to awaken us to having been seized by love for every creature.

---

4. White, "The Historical Roots," p. 1207. White, a medieval historian who specialized in technology and culture, evidently did not notice that there were two creation narratives at the beginning of Genesis.

2. Anthropocentrism and the Adam-and-Eve Narrative

Before beginning to unfold my interpretation of the seven-days narrative, let me note that it is possible to read the Adam-and-Eve narrative wholly within the parameters of an anthropocentric spirituality. It is possible, from an anthropocentric perspective, to read the Adam-and-Eve call to stewardship as a call to be stewards because that is essential to the well-being of present and future *humans*. That is, the call to stewardship can be read as a call to preserve resources for our grandchildren and their grandchildren after them. As long as this remains inclusive of all humans, it is more than enlightened selfishness; but it remains anthropocentric because it presumes that only humans are subjects of moral concern. In this way the Adam-and-Eve narrative can be subsumed within a spirituality that is indeed concerned with good stewardship of the environment but remains wholly anthropocentric.

Such anthropocentrism haunts the framing rhetoric of modern Western environmentalism. Consider, for instance, the grammar of the very word "environmentalism." Typically "environmentalism" is understood to refer to humanity's environment. That is, it refers to all flora and fauna *except humans*. We are not part of the environment; the environment is what surrounds and sustains us humans, and we are concerned if it is threatened because that poses a threat to us. In this way, the word "environmentalism" surreptitiously erases all nonhuman others as subjects of moral concern.

As long as such anthropocentric environmentalism remains inclusive of all humans it is, again, more than enlightened selfishness. But it remains anthropocentric and thus does not qualify as true creation spirituality, for it elides all nonhuman creatures from the sphere of our spiritual concern. By contrast, in the seven-days-of-Creation narrative God delights in all creatures. Because the Adam-and-Eve narrative is susceptible to anthropocentric interpretation, it is crucial that it be read (as the final redactors of the primeval history wisely arranged it) within the context of the wholly awakened creation spirituality of the seven-days-of-Creation narrative, for then the call to be good stewards of creation comes in the immediate awakening of having been seized by love for every creature.

In summary, the Adam-and-Eve narrative is protected from anthropocentric appropriation and enfolded within the spiritual dynamics of the final redaction of the primeval history by its placement immediately after the seven-days narrative.[5] Within the overall structure of the primeval history as it finally developed, the Adam-and-Eve narrative calls us to be good stewards of God's garden in response to our having been seized by love for all creatures.[6]

3. The Seven-Days Narrative: A Wholly Peaceable Creation

Predominant modern interpretations of the seven-days narrative overwhelmingly emphasize the creation of humans in the image of God, the blessing of humans, and the call for humans to subdue the earth and have dominion over all creatures on earth. These are clearly significant emphases in the seven-days narrative; but it is crucial to remember that they are all clustered together in the space of only a few lines within a much longer narrative. The creation of humans occupies only the latter half of Day Six in the narrative of the seven days. So the exegetical rush to the creation of humans does violence to the majestic prose with which this narrative luxuriates in every day of creating.

On the first five days of creating, God creates the night and the day, oceans and dry land, plants and birds and fish. God is pictured rejoicing in

5. Again, the Adam-and-Eve narrative is centuries older than the seven-days narrative. The seven-days narrative in its extant form, along with the primeval history as a whole, most likely dates to the end of — or immediately after the end of — the Israelites' period of exile.

6. Among Christian scholars, the interpretation of the seven-days-of-Creation narrative I am arguing for remains marginal, but it is steadily gaining recognition and is even, I suspect, rapidly on its way to becoming the new mainstream view. For one notable, very early advocate of the kind of reading of dominion that I am advocating, see Walter Brueggemann, *Genesis*, Interpretation: A Bible Commentary for Teaching and Preaching, ed. Patrick Miller (Atlanta: John Knox Press, 1982). On a positive but more ambiguous note, see Bernard Anderson, *From Creation to New Creation* (Minneapolis: Fortress, 1994). Finally, for work that not only supports my reading but marks a serious turning point vis-à-vis attention to creation in Christian biblical studies (if not quite yet a serious turning point vis-à-vis attention to nonhuman creatures), see Terence E. Fretheim, *God and World in the Old Testament: A Relational Theology of Creation* (Nashville: Abingdon, 2005).

creation. Again and again we hear, "It was good," "It was good." In Hebrew the "it was good" signals not dispassionate evaluation but delight. It is the delight with which one is filled when one is swept up in a beautiful sunset, awestruck by a full dome of brilliant stars, soothed by lapping waves on a sandy shore, or smilingly seized by the play of sea otters, horses, kittens, or happy children.

God not only delights in creation and in all creatures, but God blesses all creatures. In the ancient Hebrew context, blessings are highly significant. Quite rightly, then, tremendous emphasis has been placed on God's famous blessing of humans. Yet there is another blessing in the seven-days narrative that even many scholarly commentaries overlook. God also explicitly blesses the birds and the fishes, calling on them to also be fruitful and multiply: "And God saw that it was good. God blessed them, saying, 'Be fruitful and multiply and fill the waters in the seas, and let birds multiply on the earth'" (Gen. 1:22). In the Flood narrative, as we have seen, this blessing of the fish and birds is explicitly broadened with a blessing of all land animals (Gen. 8:17).

At the beginning of the sixth and final day of creating, God speaks, and the earth brings forth creatures of every kind, cattle and creeping things and wild animals. Here again, God delights: "God saw that it was good." Then comes the famous "in our image," "subdue," and "have dominion" passage:

> Then God said, "Let us make humankind in our image, according to our likeness; and let them have dominion over the fish of the sea, and over the birds of the air, and over the cattle, and over all the wild animals of the earth, and over every creeping thing that creeps upon the earth." So God created humankind in his image, in the image of God he created them; male and female he created them. God blessed them, and God said to them, "Be fruitful and multiply, and fill the earth and subdue it; and have dominion over the fish of the sea and over the birds of the air and over every living thing that moves upon the earth." (Gen. 1:26-28)

These are some of the best-known verses in all of the Jewish or Christian scriptures. Until recently, however, very few people have noticed the very next verses:

God said, "See, I have given you every plant yielding seed that is upon the face of all the earth, and every tree with seed in its fruit; you shall have them for food. And to every beast of the earth, and to every bird of the air, and to everything that creeps on the earth, everything that has the breath of life, I have given every green plant for food." And it was so. God saw everything that he had made, and indeed, it was very good. (Gen. 1:29-31)

There is no ambiguity here: we were given plants and fruits for food, and so were all other creatures with "the breath of life" in them. No creature is given any animal for food. In fact, the passage is not only explicitly vegetarian, it tilts toward the fructarian, for the emphasis on seeds and fruit suggests that in this harmonious creation not even plants would be destroyed for food; only their fruit and seeds would be harvested.

This vision of a wholly peaceable creation is hopelessly unrealistic, hopelessly idealistic. But it was not written out of ignorance. Again, this is not a stunningly bad stab at doing science. No people have ever done science quite this badly (i.e., looked around and concluded that the world is fructarian). The ancient Israelites lived in wilderness under conditions in which most modern Westerners would struggle simply to survive. They were intimately and brutally aware of the basics about how the real natural world worked. Moreover, this passage reached its received written form while the Israelites were in captivity in Babylon. As a people attacked, defeated, and forcibly marched from their homeland and into captivity, these Israelites were also intimately and brutally aware of how the real political world works.

The ancient Israelites were fully aware of the harsh realities afflicting all creatures in creation. And they were fully aware of the harsh suffering and injustice suffusing social and political relations. Nonetheless, they refused to compromise their hope and vision of a perfectly beautiful world where all creatures live delightful lives in perfect harmony. Precisely in the midst of defeat and suffering, and with infinite sensitivity to every creature, the ancient Israelites bore witness to this incredible, utterly unrealistic, wondrous vision of a perfectly peaceful and harmonious world.

Indeed, the Israelites offered up a vision of a perfectly beautiful world not only as a vision of creation as God first intended it, but also of creation as God *ultimately* intends it. For this same hope is proclaimed in a famous eschatological passage in Isaiah. In this passage, most likely written while the Israelites were living in forced exile in Babylon, the Israelites nonetheless proclaimed their faith in a day when a righteous judge would come and bring justice and right relationships among all peoples. Not only that, but with that heightened sensitivity to others' suffering that one's own suffering can bring, the vision of the Israelites extended beyond human concerns. The Isaiah passage ends with the famous "lion and lamb" vision of the peaceable creation:

> The wolf shall live with the lamb, the leopard shall lie down with the kid, the calf and the lion and the fatling together, and a little child shall lead them. The cow and the bear shall graze, their young shall lie down together; and the lion shall eat straw like the ox. The nursing child shall play over the hole of the asp, and the weaned child shall put its hand in the adder's den. They will not hurt or destroy on all my holy mountain; for the earth will be full of the knowledge of the Lord as the waters cover the sea. (Isa. 11:6-9)

Again, the ancient Israelites were brutally aware of how both the real political and natural worlds work. Yet, embroiled in precisely such brutal realities, they offered up as what is primordial and ultimate — alpha and omega, "in the beginning" and "in the end," before all, above all, beyond all — a delightful, utterly unrealistic, wondrous vision of a wholly peaceable world.

4. Profoundly and Deliberately Unrealistic

The final authors/redactors of the seven-days-of-Creation narrative offer up a vision of a perfectly beautiful and harmonious creation. This, they proclaim, is the creation a God of love would desire and have: a wondrous, peaceable world where all creatures live blessed lives in perfect harmony. Of course, for us to realize in our world the reality of the peaceable creation as it is pictured in the seven-days-of-Creation narrative is impossible. It is not possible for us to live, at a micro-biotic level even to breathe, without killing.

Because the vision of the narrative is of a perfectly beautiful and harmonious peaceable creation, the Christian notion of the Fall, which is typically associated with the Adam-and-Eve narrative (i.e., where Adam and Eve are exiled from the Garden of Eden), is actually much more clear with respect to the seven-days narrative. For the stark contrast between the seven-days vision of God's peaceable world and the sufferings and horrors that fill our real world makes our primordial sense for the fallenness of our world (i.e., for the reality of the suffering and injustice suffusing creation) instant and searing. We first come to awareness that is already and inextricably complicit. We are fallen. Those who dismiss the vision of the seven-days-of-Creation narrative because it is hopelessly unrealistic forget that the ancient Israelites were intimately aware of the brutal realities of our world. The contrast with reality is deliberate and precisely the point. It is an audacious proclamation of the alpha and omega of love made eyes wide open to the suffering and injustice that suffuse creation.

As evidenced in the brutal picture of the world just before the rainbow covenant (i.e., a world of dread, murder, and capital punishment — a world no better than the one described just before the Flood), the final redactors/authors of the seven-days narrative are fully aware of the character of our world and are realistic about its possibilities. Again, they live without any modern defenses against disease, wild animals, and weather, and they write out of a context of attack, defeat, and exile. They are fully aware that the perfectly peaceable world is an impossible dream. But they refuse to allow practical realism to force denial of their moral ideals. And as I have explained already — and will explore further below — it is the ancient Israelites' conviction about the primordial and ultimate priority of love, a conviction realized amid severe real-world oppression and suffering, and articulated most profoundly in the story of how the God of grace is born in reaction to the horrors of the Flood — it is this conviction that inspires the vision of the seven days of Creation.

As a result, in stark contrast to those who would have us bow to reality interpreted in wholly materialist terms, the primeval history calls us to remain utterly faithful to a hopelessly idealistic vision of the world, to a vision of the world as a wholly gracious God would have it, while at the same time remaining brutally realistic about the character of and extant possibilities for our world, that is, while at the same time naming and owning that we and our world are fallen, inextricably bound up in a world suffused with injustice, violence, and suffering.

Note that the impossibility of achieving the peaceable ideal is no more an excuse to abuse creation than the impossibility of being sinless is an excuse for doing wrong, or the impossibility of eliminating all suffering, poverty, injustice, or sickness is a reason to remain inert in the face of suffering, poverty, injustice or sickness. Despite the impossibility of ultimate success, morally awakened people of diverse faiths have through the ages struggled against suffering, poverty, injustice, and sickness (e.g., have fed the hungry, clothed the poor, comforted the sick, and visited those persecuted and imprisoned).

With the same passion, the seven-days-of-Creation narrative, with breathtaking sensitivity to all suffering and to all creatures, calls on us to struggle and sacrifice in the present, to live as lovingly as possible, and to strive to realize perfect love's intentions as fully as possible for every creature on earth — whether perfection is achievable or not. In ways I will delineate more precisely below, the seven-days narrative strives to awaken us to having been seized by love for all creatures, and so to awaken us to the living source of a passion to live toward the impossible dream of a wholly peaceable world.

In sum, the authors/redactors of the primeval history are realistic about real-world moral potentials. But they refuse to allow practical realism to force them to deny or compromise the full reality of their having been seized by love for all creatures. The primeval history is wholly realistic about both our most profound moral ideals and the brutal aspects of the reality we inhabit. According to the primeval history, we come to awareness already and inextricably complicit. That we are fallen means that we are inescapably caught in the maw of the abyss (i.e., we are inescapably caught up in all the suffering and injustice, we are inescapably embedded within this vale of tears). At the same time, in our received Genesis version of the Flood narrative, the primeval history proclaims that despite our complicity, despite even the fact that the "human heart is evil from youth," and despite the awful realities of the world, love is primordial and ultimate. Indeed, as I will detail below, it is that conviction in all its unmitigated fullness and wonder that is the inspiration and point of the seven-days narrative.

By now it is clear that the first Creation narrative is not a stunningly bad stab at doing science but a stunningly optimistic proclamation concerning God's ideals and love for creation. Far from being an invitation to wrest the rest of creation to our own purposes and interests, the seven-days-of-Creation narrative offers up a religious and moral ideal, affirming the gracious character of God and naming what is good and, by contrast, what is evil. Thus this narrative suggests an ethical orientation within the world, one that directs our sympathies, ideals, and actions. At this point I could already conclude that the peaceable world pictured in the seven-days narrative provides us with an ideal, and as such it might be seen as a blueprint, a guide to righteousness, a basis for Jewish and Christian ethics regarding our care of creation.

While not inaccurate, such a reading of the text would remain radically incomplete and spiritually superficial — "spiritually superficial" because, taken as a "blueprint," the text would serve as an external authority to be obeyed, not as a source of spiritual awakening; "radically incomplete" because I appear to have dodged some pivotal passages: What about, for example, our creation in God's image (the *imago dei*)? What about the commands to "subdue" and to "have dominion"? Have I not read this text selectively, quietly ignoring the verses that create a problem for my ecological and creature-loving interests? Yes indeed, so far I have. Significantly, however, it is precisely when one attends to the *imago dei*, the "subdue," and the "have dominion" commands, that the full spiritual profundity of the seven-days-of-Creation narrative becomes apparent. For then it becomes even more clear that the seven-days narrative is *not* a utopian blueprint, not a basis for constructing a religious ethic, not a ground from which one can (modern style) deduce a set of ethical rules that should be obeyed; rather, it is an astounding, spiritually profound testimony that strives to awaken us to having been seized by love for all the creatures that surround us — and thus inspiring us toward loving and life-affirming being in the world.

5. Domination

As is by now clear, God delights in every creature in a blessed and harmonious world in the seven-days narrative. Thus does the seven-days narrative powerfully affirm the value of every creature and of all creation. But, what about the creation of humans in the image of God? What about the command to subdue the earth and to have dominion over every creature on earth? Don't these parts of the seven-days narrative mean to affirm beyond any question humanity's absolute right to control and use all other creatures and all the rest of creation? It will become clear that the answer to this question is "no." But in the modern period the "domination" interpretation came to be seen as quite obviously the true teaching of the seven-days narrative. This understanding remains widespread and powerful, so I will take a few moments to unfold a common (if rarely made explicit) way of framing the passage that facilitates the "domination" misreading.

It has been common to imagine that the seven-days-of-Creation narrative paints a very particular vision of creation. Humans are on top; a hard line separates humans from animals; a hierarchy orders the various species of animals, from chimpanzees and dolphins up top descending through a continuum on down to worms and so forth; a soft line is placed between animals and plants, and then a fairly hard line separates the animate from the inanimate.

This is obviously a legitimate hierarchy in terms of intelligence, culture, and language.[7] But one should remember what Albert Schweitzer reportedly quipped about hierarchies: the interesting thing is that those making the hierarchy tend to end up on top. That does not mean that one should throw out all hierarchical thinking. Hierarchies pervade reality. Many rightly reflect important differences in levels of expertise or wisdom, and systemic denial of them only blinds one to powerful and often significant aspects of biological and sociopolitical reality.

It does no good to deny the hierarchies that quite reasonably put us on top sociopolitically or conceptually, but it is important not to make those hierarchies exclusive and absolute. There are other relevant hierarchies

---

7. Whatever may be the capacity or set of capacities to which the *imago dei* refers (the debate is endless), it is clearly some kind of reference to our obvious and incredible superiority over all other earthly creatures. Other creatures are indeed amazing, and some evidently have capacities for language, empathy, culture, and reasoning that we are only beginning to appreciate. But no other species is even close to composing poetry, philosophizing, being ethical, or analyzing rock samples on Mars.

to keep in mind. Indeed, at certain moments the recognition of other hierarchies can be vitally important. For instance, if you are out sailing in shark-filled waters and an unexpected jolt throws you into the water with the sharks, it would be very good if another hierarchy — one involving strength, size, excellence in swimming, and teeth — were immediately made primary (this tends to happen automatically).

Such examples could easily be multiplied. Obviously, in multiple contexts all kinds of hierarchies, and usually more than one at once, are relevant. Note that none of the hierarchies mentioned thus far — not the standard sociocultural hierarchy, nor the conceptual capacity hierarchy, nor the human/shark-in-water hierarchy — is particularly spiritual. What might a distinctly spiritual hierarchy look like? A central Christian category, one with analogues across other faiths, would be "sinfulness/purity." What happens if we use this spiritually significant category to organize the hierarchy? Its order reverses. Precisely the potentials for language, intelligence, and culture that put us at the top of one hierarchy put us at the bottom of the other. I am convinced I have had dogs with some capacity for sin, but be that as it may, in comparison to trees, worms, cats, and chimps, we are by far the most sinful aspect of creation.

Christians can think of this with respect to the idea of incarnation, that is, with respect to the idea of the Word becoming flesh. That is, it would be helpful to see God's total embrace of humanity not merely as God dipping into the top of creation, becoming one of us (which, we like to think, could not be that bad!), but to see the incarnation as God's loving, sacrificial, kenotic identification and embrace of the most distant, the most sinful, the most alien part of creation — *humans*. In thus proclaiming divinity's most intimate unifying embrace of the furthermost limit of creation, humans, the doctrine of the incarnation proclaims that all the rest of creation, which is relatively near, lies within the all-encompassing embrace of divine grace.

But the problem with the domination reading of the seven-days narrative is subtler than the absolutizing of a hierarchy. Again, it has been common to think that the seven-days narrative teaches that God created humans in God's image so that we may rule the earth. That is, humans should dominate the earth because God said so. But as is clear once we free ourselves of anthropocentric prejudice, this is most definitely not the teaching of the seven-days narrative. The problem with the anthropocentric reading is that it displaces nonhuman creatures as a subject of direct divine concern. On this reading, God's primary focus is humans, and God's primary role lies in authorizing human domination of all the rest of creation. Moreover, the prime division read into the narrative is placed between humans and animals. Vis-à-vis animals and the rest of creation, God is subtly displaced as humanity's God-like status above all the rest of creation is emphasized.

God is not displaced in the seven-days-of-Creation narrative. On the contrary, the seven-days narrative is clearly and continually focused, day after day after day, on God's creative activity, on God's delight in all creatures and all creation, on God's blessing of and love for all creatures, and last, on God's rest on the seventh day. The prime division in the first Creation narrative is not between humans and animals, but between the Creator and all creatures (including humans, who are one kind of creature).[8] We humans are not at the center of the seven-days narrative; God is at the center of the seven-days narrative. The seven-days narrative is not about establishing the preeminence of humans but about proclaiming the preeminence and love of God, who would have all creatures live blessed lives in a perfectly delightful world.

The seven-days-of-Creation narrative is primarily about proclaiming the reality and character of the dominion of God. And let us be perfectly clear about the stunning affirmation implicit in the seven-days vision of a perfectly beautiful and harmonious world in which all creation delights God, in which all creatures bring God joy, and in which all creatures are blessed *by* God. This is a way of proclaiming that God has been seized by love for every creature.

---

8. Note how the pertinent ancient Hebrew categories (i.e., Creator, creation, creatures, kinds of creatures) map out (ontological) spheres fundamentally different from the common modern categories (i.e., Creator, nature, humans, animals). This mapping is another aspect of the systemic distortions permeating modern Western language and reason at the most fundamental level. And, as I discussed in early parts of this work, these distortions contribute to the betrayal of our love, and thus to a betrayal of our morality and ethics.

6. Dominion

Once we remind ourselves that this narrative is primarily concerned with proclaiming the reality and character of the dominion of God, three questions come into view. Taken together, they utterly displace the "domination" interpretation of the *imago dei* (i.e., "subdue" and "have dominion") and reveal the true character of dominion.[9] Here is the first of the three questions: "Who in the seven-days narrative has absolute authority, absolute sovereignty, absolute dominion, absolute rule?" The answer is almost too obvious to state: God.

Here is the second of the three questions: What is the character of God's subduing of the chaos? What is the character of God's absolute authority, God's absolute rule? What is the character of Godly dominion? The answer to these questions is also completely clear: God's dominion is wholly and perfectly loving. God delights in all creatures and all creation, and God blesses and thereby expresses divine love for and desire for the flourishing and happiness of every creature. The expressly vegetarian (and likely fructarian) provision for food makes clear God's desire that absolute and utter peace would fill the earth, that all creatures might live wonderful lives in perfect harmony. In short, God is seized by love for creatures of every kind, and God is seized by love for creatures (including humans) that are less than perfect and less powerful and lower than God.

When I preach on this passage, I always step out from behind the pulpit and say, "If a single image could convey the picture of God's dominion in the seven-days-of-Creation narrative, it would be this," and then I bow deeply and open and extend my arms downward and outward in a gesture

9. It has been common for scholars to attempt to qualify the meaning of "dominion" in the context of the *imago dei* by relating our creation in the image of God to the ancient practice of a king appointing a viceroy to act in his stead as a ruler in a distant city, the idea being that we have been appointed to be God's representative and thus should rule in accord with God's command. My approach here is not at all in conflict with this move, which is helpful and which has largely resisted interpretations that foster exploitation. But I am seeking to make clear that the character of dominion in the context of the *imago dei* is more concretely defined within the dynamics of the seven-days-of-Creation narrative itself than has been commonly recognized.

of giving and caring; and then I sweep my arms up and together in a gesture of loving embrace.

All this expresses how God's act of creation, the act of bringing creatures into autonomous being, of delighting in and blessing all creatures, has always been understood theologically as the original and originating act of love, wherein the lives of all creatures, including those of us humans, are acknowledged primarily and ultimately as gifts of a loving God. This profound dimension of the seven-days-of-Creation narrative unfolds and testifies to the pivotal realization of the Flood narrative: divine love, gracious love, is primordial and ultimate, and the be-ing of every creature, including us humans, is in reality — primordially and ultimately — a gift.

Christians can discern here a deep continuity between the spiritual dynamics inspiring the doctrines of creation and incarnation. For if in Creation, God's characteristic stance is a bowing down, an affirmation of and joy in all that is below, a kenotic love for all creation and all creatures, then the incarnation is the radical completion of the same logic, the Creator's total and radically intimate identification with the creaturely — the Word become *flesh* — in love.

Now for the third question. To review, the first question was: Who subdues and rules absolutely? The answer: God. The second question was: What is the character of God's absolute dominion? The answer: It is loving, caring, being concerned. The third question follows immediately: If this is the character of God's dominion, and if we are rightly to live out our creation in the image of God, if we — insofar as we have dominion over all creatures — are to mirror God's dominion over all creatures, what will be the character of our subduing of the earth, and what will be the character of our dominion over other creatures?[10]

Once again, the answer is obvious. If the God who is infinitely above us in power, perfection, intelligence, purity, and goodness bows down in

---

10. To reiterate, I am taking no particular stand on the meaning of the *imago dei*, which remains the subject of debate. My concern is with the character of the "subdue" and "have dominion," the meaning of which, I am arguing, is in fact very clearly defined within the overall structure of the narrative: this immediate textual meaning is not only more profound but far more certain than understandings derived from what are inevitably more general philological or sociocultural appeals.

gracious love to all who are absolutely other than God, even to us humans in our sinfulness — if that is the character of God's dominion, if that is the nature of the love divine that we confess, celebrate, and hope in — then we truly realize the divine spirit of dominion when we, too, act out of our love for all others, including our love for those who are different in kind (as we are different from God) and who are below us in power, intelligence, and even goodness.

Inspired by the Spirit, we will love as God loves; we will be filled with joy when others (*all* others) flourish; we will mourn when they suffer; we will enable, protect, empower, provide, and sacrifice out of love for every creature. And just as God, having been seized by love for all creatures, subdued the chaos in order to make places — seas, skies, mountains, rivers, plains — in which all creatures might find delight, sustenance, and a home, so we faithfully imitate God when we, too, awakened by love for every creature, subdue the earth by preserving places — seas, skies, mountains, rivers, plains — in which all creatures, including humans, might find delight, sustenance, and a home. In summary, insofar as we are filled and inspired by the Spirit, which is to say, insofar as we are awake to all the life that surrounds us, insofar as we have been seized by love for every creature, our rule and dominion will be formed by love and we will strive, insofar as is humanly possible, toward perfect realization of divine peace on earth.

It is crucial that we open ourselves to the spiritual call of the narrative. The seven-days narrative is not trying to set forth a command that must be obeyed. Inspired by the Spirit of love, the Spirit of having been seized, it is attempting to awaken us to that same Spirit, to open us to the full breadth and depth of divine love. I especially enjoy preaching on the true spirit of Godly dominion over all other creatures because after the sermon I am always privileged to be regaled by numerous stories about the joy and delight people have taken in all sorts of creatures. Some stories are happy, some tragic, some are confessions, some are expressions of grief, but all are wonderful, touching, loving, and full of the true spirit of dominion. Some stories are as fresh as that day; some are fifty and sixty years old, memories treasured silently and privately until serious permission to share was given.

These stories reflect profound spiritual realities and riches that predominant streams of modern rationalities and Jewish and Christian theologies have to a large degree effectively suppressed, to devastating effect, for decades. The devastating "domination" misreading of the seven-days-of-Creation narrative, which became predominant in the twentieth century, has empowered a perverse and truncated spirituality that gets the revelation of the seven-days narrative exactly backwards and keeps us from owning and proclaiming the full depth and breadth of the love of God. The standard modern interpretation equates dominion with domination. It replaces having been seized by love for all creatures with love of the *use and appropriation of other creatures*. It replaces delight in other creatures' delights with delight in using and appropriating them. The standard modern interpretation, long common in conservative and liberal churches alike, and also shared by materialist critics of the seven-days narrative, is an abusive misreading of the seven-days-of-Creation narrative's clear spiritual teaching.

The seven-days-of-Creation narrative does not strive to inspire a spirit of superiority, of distance, of domination, or of exploitation. The seven-days narrative is inspired by, testifies to, and hopes to inspire a spirit immediately seized by divine love, that is, to awaken us to having been seized by love for *every* other, to inspire us to a spirit of love, of affirmation, of care. The narrative dares to affirm and celebrate, without any qualification or dampening, our infinite concern and love for every one of God's beloved creatures. For the seven-days narrative calls us to love as God loves. It calls us to Godly dominion.

7. To Love as God Loves

By this point it is clear how the seven-days-of-Creation narrative's call to dominion protects us from any interpretation of the Adam-and-Eve narrative that yields the sort of truncated spirituality one finds even among many (though certainly not all) environmentalists. The spirituality can be truncated insofar as concern for the environment is rooted solely in concern for humans (or, far worse, in concern for me and mine), while all other creatures are relegated to the status of anonymous thing-hood, parts and pieces of the eco-"system" that constitutes humans' environment.

The profound dominion testimony of the seven-days narrative has been elided by the domination reading for so long that I will belabor it. If the seven-days-of-Creation narrative testifies that the God who is infinitely above us in power, perfection, intelligence, purity, and goodness still bows down in love to that which is absolutely other than God, even (taking into account the realism of the Flood narrative) to us humans in our sinfulness, if that is the character of God's spirituality, the character of God's dominion, if that is the nature of the love divine that one confesses, celebrates, and hopes in, then what, according to the seven-days narrative, should be our spiritual orientation toward all those who are beneath us in power, intelligence, and goodness, who are relatively other to us?

To make the point vivid: If that is God's spiritual orientation toward humans and all other creatures, if that is the spiritual orientation that we confess as divine, then what should our spiritual orientation be toward a cockroach? The answer of the seven-days-of-Creation narrative is utterly clear: We truly reflect our creation in the image of God, we love as God loves, when we *love* the cockroach.

We reflect the image of God when we are wholly and without qualification seized by love for the cockroach and for every creature, every flower of the field, every sparrow, every human. In the purity of the transcendent, having been seized by love for the cockroach, our love is absolute and unqualified. In the transcending moment there is no distinction between the cockroach and any other creature. Since this love is gracious, not based on merit, there is no distinction between the cockroach and me with respect to God's infinite love. In the moment in which our attention is directed to a single other and we are seized by love for that particular cockroach, or that particular cat or dog, or some animal struck and writhing in its death throes on the street, our love is absolute and unqualified.

To be clear, such situations are abstractions from most daily reality, for usually we are forced to choose among multiple others in situations where our fidelity to one creature or another must be compromised. In situations where our options are limited and choices must be made among beloved others — this is the sphere of ethics — I would argue that if there are significant distinctions among others, then they should be brought into consideration. For instance, if we were to face an either/or decision between saving a cockroach or a human, then, all other factors being equal, we most definitely *should* save the human. But we should never forget that we have been forced to draw an ethical distinction that requires the violation of our love for the cockroach. We mourn the cockroach, and we realize that we have been forced in a fallen world, where only bad choices present themselves, to choose the lesser of two evils. In the wake of such situations, which pervade our daily lives, those fully alive to having been seized by love for all creatures gain through such experiences a visceral sense for why, through our tears, we call this world fallen.

However, the seven-days-of-Creation narrative, as I will discuss in more detail below, is operating in a supraethical realm, so such ethical considerations are not in play. In the seven-days narrative, no ethical distinctions are drawn with regard to God's love for creatures. God loves every creature absolutely, without regard for merit, which is to say, God's love is constant, universal, and gracious. We humans are undeniably set apart in the seven-days narrative as superior in definitive respects (e.g., in terms of intelligence); but as is now clear, the fact that we are superior in certain respects provides no basis for any claim that we are — or deserve to be — loved more by God. For love is not predicated on merit or any economy of return. Our superiority provides a basis for the ascription of the responsibility for dominion and for subduing the earth. It does not establish a special privilege that legitimates human domination. To the contrary, we reflect the image of God when we love as God loves, when we are seized by love for every creature.

8. "Subdue"

Note that this understanding of the dominion of love guides us in understanding how and for whom we are called to subdue the earth. In the first Creation account, God brings forth the peaceable world by subduing chaos for the good of all creatures. We are called — in imitation of God — to subdue the chaos that continually afflicts the earth, to subdue chaos on earth toward a more perfect realization of Godly dominion, to subdue our chaotic world toward a more complete realization of God's peaceable world. The "subdue" and "have dominion," then, are both calls to work, through the impossible, toward a realization of peace on earth.

In summary, the seven-days narrative portrays God as subduing chaos for the sake of all creatures, and portrays God as lovingly embracing, blessing, and providing for all creatures. Most Christians (among many others) in the last few centuries have adopted a very different posture. Their "domination" stance found support in the predominant modern reading of the seven-days narrative. That predominant reading urged Christians to think of "dominion," "rule," and "subdue" in terms of traits that characterize those we condemn as tyrants. By now it should be clear that that predominant modern interpretation is profoundly mistaken. With stunning clarity and unmitigated sensitivity, the seven-days narrative does more than call on us to be stewards of creation (as in the chronologically earlier Adam-and-Eve narrative), for in radical fashion the seven-days narrative testifies to love for every creature and thereby seeks to awaken in us love for every creature.

The seven-days-of-Creation narrative is inspired by, testifies to, and hopes to inspire a spirit immediately seized by divine love, that is, to awaken us to having been seized by love for every creature. The seven-days narrative, then, does not suggest that we should be obedient to any external authority. It does not want us to act out of obedience to some articulated command of God. It does not want us to act out of obedience to the dictates of a canonical text. It does not even expect or want us to act out of obedience. It strives to awaken us to having been seized by love for every creature. And it expects us to act in response to having been seized by this love.

In order to be awakened with accuracy and depth in the spirituality of this narrative, in order to gain insight concerning its testimony about the character of God's twofold relationship with all creatures (namely, God's delight in all creatures and, more profoundly, God's love for every creature), and in order to be seized with accuracy and depth by the spirituality of this narrative, we should bring to mind the delight and love we have experienced when we have been seized by love for other creatures (including, of course, other people). That is, in order to be awakened by and to the spirituality of the narrative, we need to luxuriate in its wondrous vision of a wholly peaceable world, and we need to allow ourselves to imagine and to be seized by a wondrous vision of love that is perfect, all-encompassing, and fully realized.

Contrary to the spirituality encouraged by the domination misreading, the spirituality of the Flood and seven-days narratives is not a spirituality of superiority, of distance, of domination, or of exploitation. It is a spirituality of love, of affirmation, and of care. It is a spirituality that dares to affirm, celebrate, and proclaim — without any qualification or dampening — our infinite sensitivity to every other being.

We should note that, in the light of one's recognition of and opening to having been seized by love for every creature, the searing contrast between the joy and communion one would have with these creatures, on the one hand, and the reality of life in this vale of tears, on the other hand (i.e., our sense of the fallenness of the world), becomes palpable. Indeed, our sense of the fallenness of the world is heightened in direct proportion to our awakening to passionate desire for a perfectly beautiful and harmonious world in which no creature, no life, no matter how small or seemingly insignificant, is violated. At this juncture, where affirmation that gracious love is ultimate and primordial is conjoined with searing awareness of all the injustice, pain, and suffering that suffuse reality (in theological terms, the searing awareness that our world is fallen), the full complexity and spiritual profundity of the primeval history, and the critical insights that distinguish it from the Enuma Elish and Hobbesian Darwinism, come fully into view.

CHAPTER SEVEN

Dominion versus Domination

Living Life and Living Death

1. Rural Wisdom

People sometimes expect that, because of the fructarian ideal so power-fully affirmed in the seven-days-of-Creation narrative, I meet with resis-tance to this spirituality from farmers, ranchers, and other rural folks. On the contrary, as I have shared these ideas in churches in rural areas around the country, I have consistently found the opposite to be the norm. This affirmation of rural folks resonates not only with the stories of my many students from rural settings but also with my own country upbringing. I didn't grow up on a farm, but I grew up in a rural town of 1,500 in dairy country. We were all aware of how people treated their animals and their land, and we judged them accordingly. Moreover, we knew that the way people treated their farm or ranch animals told us a great deal about how those same people were likely to treat other people. Even in cities and sub-urbs, who admires (or wholly trusts) neighbors who mistreat their pets?

At the turn of the millennium, I heard a Midwestern pig farmer inter-viewed about factory farms on National Public Radio.[1] George Burge was eighty-four and long since retired, but he was animated about his old pigs, and he hated factory "farms." The interviewer, John McChesney, noted

1. All quotations come from an e-mail transcript of National Public Radio's *All Things Considered* series, "The Changing Face of America." Story reported by John McChesney, originally aired on Sept. 27, 2000. Transcript produced by Burrelle's In-formation Services, Box 7, Livingston, NJ 07039.

that Mr. Burge's eyes misted as he recounted the story of one old mother pig, Pug. Mr. Burge had built a nest inside a shed so Pug could give birth to her litter. When he went out one night he discovered that she had instead built her own grass nest outside the shed. Mr. Burge said:

> She come up there to me, went to loving on me, just a-grunting. I says, "Pug, damn it, you're supposed to go in the shed." And she'd look at me and rub on me. And I fooled around with her and scratched her tits a little bit and scratched her behind the ears. And finally I got her tail and I slapped her butt and I says, "Get your ass in that shed." And, my gosh, she just walked on into bed. I shut the door, and the next morning went down there and she had ten, eleven pigs laying there.

At this point, McChesney breaks away, noting pointedly that those piglets were being raised for the slaughterhouse. So where, he wonders, does that leave the complaint about factory "farms"? McChesney allows a plain-speaking country lawyer, George Huff, to respond: "Between birth and death there's life," says Huff, "and it makes a difference how you treat animals when they're alive."

Far from being marginal, and despite humans' corporate and self-interested willingness to avoid thinking about the treatment of animals in places like factory "farms," Mr. Burge and Mr. Huff's moral apprehensions reflect overwhelmingly common real-world thinking about the mistreatment of animals. Their moral wisdom about the mistreatment of animals is also shared by modern rural folks, and, it is now clear, by the ancient Israelites (who were also rural by modern standards).

Such rural wisdom instinctively distinguishes between dominion and domination, which, I will argue, amounts to the difference between living life and living death. As such, it offers a decisive rejoinder to the anomie (despair over a life that seems meaningless), nihilism (the assertion that life *is* meaningless), and solipsism (a belief in the primordial isolation of the atomistic self, of the Cartesian "I") that infamously plague modern Western rationality. It turns out that it is no accident that rural folks live in an enchanted world while those "enlightened" by materialism live in a world that appears to them to be wholly disenchanted precisely because they insist on filtering their vision wholesale through materialist lenses.

2. The Essential Paradox in Friendship
and the Logic of Domination

The secret of this rural moral wisdom (where "moral wisdom" names the wisdom that flows from having been seized by love for all creatures) can be explained in light of the essential paradox in friendship. True and fast friends are good to have in one's life. But friendship is characterized by living for the other, love for the other. Paradoxically, then, we receive the good of friendship only to the degree that we do not pursue the friendship for *ourselves* but for the *other*. This is why, for instance, if you discover that someone has been acting as your friend solely for the sake of making a connection or securing a promotion, that is, if that person is acting as your friend with wholly ulterior motives, you immediately conclude that he or she is not truly your friend. At the other extreme are those who have given their very lives for their friends. Most friendships fall somewhere between these two extremes, and one is fortunate to cultivate even a handful of the most precious friendships in a lifetime. But the truth of the essential paradox applies across the spectrum.

To be clear, there is nothing wrong with being friendly as you cultivate contacts and build networks; over time, some contacts may even develop into true friends. But, again, they become friends only to the degree that a real concern for the other has superseded the cultivation of the relationship for personal gain. In other words, a friendship is true to the degree that it is *not* characterized by the logic of domination, that is, to the degree that someone is not being a friend out of self-interest.

There are, it is important to remember, contexts within which the logic of domination (or, perhaps better, the absence/bracketing of the way of dominion) *may* be required, for instance, with respect to one's employer or employees (though even in those instances there is ample space for dominion). But the logic of domination should never constitute one's whole way of being or determine one's ultimate goals in the world. For to the degree that the logic of domination dictates one's relationships, one is cut off from true friendship, true love, and true community. Therefore, one is actually in peril to the degree that relationships dictated by the logic of domination fill one's life, for the endpoint of the logic of domination is spiritually devastating: utter isolation.

Therefore, to the degree that we live the logic of domination, we live a living death, for absolute success in using all relationships wholly and solely for our own interests leaves us with no true love, no genuine friends, no authentic relationships. So, while our relationships with others may sometimes appropriately involve to some limited degree the logic of domination, it is spiritually crucial to remember that, to the degree that we live the logic of domination, that is, to the degree that we live the reduction of every other creature, including other people, to the thing-to-be-appropriated-and-used, we live death.

3. The Way of Dominion

By this time the meaning of "domination" is patent; however, I should be sure to define "dominion" explicitly and precisely. "Dominion" describes loving relationships in the context of some hierarchy of power among creatures (e.g., a hierarchy pegged to health or conceptual capacity). Think, for instance, not of friends, who will typically be peers, but of the hierarchical relationship between parents and their small children. The logic of domination is evident in parents who are living out their own dreams and desires through the lives of their children. But one sees dominion where, despite a legitimate hierarchy of power and exercise of control, parents live lovingly for their children (i.e., where they live having been seized by love for their children).

Over the decades, of course, the hierarchy of power usually dissolves, and children may become peers and friends of their parents. In fact, late in the parents' lives — or due to some earlier health crisis or accident — the relationship of power may even reverse. The critical question may even become: Will the child have dominion over or exercise domination toward an infirm parent? Therefore, throughout the passage of various stages, and due to accident or illness, there may be reversals over the decades. The crucial question in this regard concerns not who has power over whom, but what is the character of the exercise of that power. What is the character of the relationship? Which prevails, the logic of domination or the way of dominion?[2]

---

2. I am gesturing very roughly here to distinctions similar to those drawn with great clarity by Martin Buber in *I and Thou*. My distinction between the logic of domi-

In summary, to live the logic of domination is to live in denial of the call of love for all others. It is to harden our hearts, to live cut off from genuine friendship and love. What I have described as moral, as loving, as having been seized by love for others, is the heart of the way of dominion, the way of true friendship and love, the way of an enchanted life full of meaningfulness, a way that brings us grief and pain over the violation of lives, and also a way that awakens us to the transcending joy of communion with other creatures, where our joy is made complete in a relationship where we have been seized by love for a creature who is simultaneously seized by love for us. In such communion we are taken up in surpassing joy, peace, fullness, satisfaction, fellowship *(koinonia)*, and delight in an enchanted world.

To the degree that we harden our hearts, we are closed off from others, closed off from transcending communion, closed off even from our own selves as beloved. So, to the degree that we live solely the logic of domination, we live a spiritually impoverished life in a disenchanted world. In short, to the degree that we live the way of dominion, we live life; and to the degree that we live the logic of domination, we live death.[3]

4. The Peril of Domination and the Spiritual Genius of the Seven-Days Narrative

Thinking again of the seven-days-of-Creation narrative, note the existential peril into which the ancient authors would have thrown God

---

nation and the logic of dominion echo the distinction Buber draws between "I-it" and "I-thou" relationships. Significantly, Buber too explicitly included all life, that is, all animals and plants, within the sphere of I-thou relationships (Martin Buber, *I and Thou*, 2nd ed., trans. R. G. Smith [New York: Charles Scribner's Sons, 1958], see esp. pp. 7-8, 23; in the more recent translation by Walter Kaufmann, *I and Thou, by Martin Buber: A New Translation with a Prologue* [New York: Simon and Schuster, 1970], see pp. 57-59, 74-75).

3. Insofar as one is seized not only by love for friends but also for strangers and even enemies, one would need to delineate other significant criteria in order to distinguish appropriately friends, family, and lovers from strangers and enemies. To articulate positively a precise understanding of "friendship" or "loves/lovers," however, would take us beyond my focus here; for my focus is on dominion in contrast to domination. In any case, the point regarding the spiritual character and consequences of living the logic of domination is clear.

if God's relationship to creation had been construed — as became predominant in modernity — in accord with the dynamics of the logic of domination. If God were portrayed to be exercising power with respect to creatures in the way assumed when one reads "domination" in place of "dominion," that is, if God were portrayed creating out of self-interest, for instance, *in order* to have relationships or *for the sake of* God's delight, then, because of the essential paradox in love and friendship, even God would suffer devastating isolation: no true love, no true friends, no true communion.

The fateful question with regard to God (i.e., with regard to proclamation about what is primordial and ultimate, what is divine) pivots on the depiction of God's exercise of power. Is God's relationship with all creatures characterized by the logic of domination or the way of dominion? The seven-days narrative is unequivocal and brilliant: it never represents God in terms of the logic of domination; God delights in all creation and blesses all creatures; God is loving, caring, giving; God thereby creates and increases value, and opens up possibilities for loving relationships. To depict God in this way is to proclaim the way of dominion as primordial and ultimate, as divine, and to name and affirm every creature as infinitely beloved.

The word "God," then, gestures to the transcending, supranaturalistic character of our having been seized by love for every creature, a love that proceeds neither from us nor from any other creature but that seizes us in relation to that creature, and, in instances where that creature is likewise awakened to us, takes us up into a transcending joy and communion (the *koinonia* where our "joy is made complete").

It is an always already preceding love — the passion of the having been seized, which proceeds neither from me nor from others — that makes the life and well-being of another a matter of infinite concern for me.[4] In

---

4. Speaking technically, I am here gesturing to what I consider to be Jean-Luc Marion's essential supplement to Levinas, namely, his explication of the givenness — from without the fourfold causation — of the gift. See esp. Jean-Luc Marion, "Sketch of a Phenomenological Concept of Gift," in Merold Westphal, ed., *Postmodern Philosophy and Christian Thought* (Bloomington: Indiana University Press, 1999), pp. 122-43. I should specify that combining the concepts of Levinas and Marion in this way is a strong move that creates an understanding different from either of their projects; I would like to

our awakening to having been seized by love for others, we find ourselves always seized by love already. This love is not the product of any desire or decision on our own part. Though we may resist it (harden our hearts), we do not initiate it. In this sense it precedes and seizes us (insofar as we do not harden our hearts). This love is not from us, nor from others, but to us for others.

Insofar as we live continually awakened to this love, we are not only seized by it but are taken up in it. We live and move and have our being in this love. Thereby we are ourselves indirectly taken up in love; we are manifest to ourselves as beloved; we know ourselves as we are seized in and by grace. This is the inspiration for and the meaning of the primordial theological confession: "God is love." This is what it means to use "God" as a sign that gestures toward the suprahuman, ever-transcending, eternal font of love, and, in accord with the seven-days narrative, to designate Creation as the act of original love, of originating love.[5]

"God" gestures to the source and character of our having been taken up in and by love, of our having been seized by every other creature. "God" names the source and character of having been seized and having been taken up by love that is full of value, meaningfulness, and joy. When the seven-days narrative proclaims the dominion of God, then, it proclaims that the way of God is the way of dominion and testifies to the ultimate, primordial, supranaturalistic source and character of the transcending

---

think, however, that it is an understanding consistent with the spirit of both of their projects, and one to which they may be receptive.

5. Insofar as this is a "love" that operates outside of every economy, it is already a love that in the context of sin will be manifest as "gracious" (e.g., as in the Flood narrative). But in ways I will detail below, insofar as the seven-days-of-Creation account depicts a perfect, moral, supraethical realm, speaking within the context of the seven-days narrative, I will refer to the primordial creative act as original and originating love, not original and originating grace. Grace is contained already within this love, though that will only become manifest in the face of sin and evil. That is, there is no intrinsic difference between "grace" and "love." But traditionally, "grace" clarifies in the context of sin that "love" is not operating on a plane where it is at all compromised or altered by sin (e.g., within an economy), and as a matter of definition, "grace" in this latter sense is perhaps inconceivable, and is in any case irrelevant within the confines of a perfect, moral, supraethical realm, such as the perfectly good creation in the seven-days narrative.

communion we find ourselves taken up in our having been seized by love for every creature.[6]

By contrast, if the seven-days narrative had portrayed God living the logic of domination as an unparalleled power over and against creation, if God had been pictured "lording it over" creation (as the predominant modern Western interpretation has had it), then God would have been belittled and impoverished, for God would have been reduced to a measure of raw power over and against the world. God as love, the God of joy and transcending communion — that God would have been lost.

In the context of such a confused domination understanding, even God would have been, because of the horrible consequences that flow from living the logic of domination, depicted as living death. For the sheer possession of power, even absolute power, in terms of a force to be exercised over and against others in accord with the logic of domination, is not only not enough to yield meaningfulness and joy, it yields precisely the opposite: utter isolation, a living death, a life devoid of joy, devoid of love, and without transcending communion (i.e., it yields a primordial solipsism that can and will deliver anomie and nihilism).

A creation narrative that proclaimed as primordial and ultimate a "God" of domination, then, would have affirmed as primordial and ultimate a living death. Is this not the devastating milieu of modern Western culture insofar as it identifies rational action with self-interested action? Is this not where the Hobbesian/Darwinian creation narrative leaves us? The

---

6. A classic theological affirmation holds that God plus the world is not more than God without the world. I am affirming the motivation behind this formulation (i.e., to emphasize that God does not create out of self-interest); but I am suggesting that it is nonetheless imprecise. The point of the formulation is to stress that God does not create out of self-interest but out of love, and thus — for the reasons delineated here — that the Creator is capable of entering into authentic loving relationships with creatures. But it is incorrect to render this point in terms of contending that God without the world is no less than God with the world. As the first creation account affirms quite explicitly, God's existence with the world is richer, more delightful, more fulfilling. The character of God's existence with the world is superior to God's existence without the world. According to the narrative (and working with the inexact categories of the narrative and of the classic theological affirmation), God is enriched and value is increased through creating, but only because God does not create in order to increase value or in order to be enriched.

seven-days narrative, forged with eyes wide open to the injustices and suffering that suffuses reality (i.e., forged amidst the realities of the Flood), and inspired by awakening to having been seized by love for every creature, strives to deliver us from such nihilistic confusion and to deliver us all into the transcending joy of having been seized by love for every creature, to deliver us to life lived in the light of a transcending love that lifts us into its gracious heights. Life lived in the light of this love is the life of faith, which is the gift of grace in the primeval history.

The key insight comes from the paradox of friendship: to gain the value of friendship, we must not engage in friendship in order to gain its value. Dominion (living out love for every other) creates value, yielding life; domination (using others for ourselves) negates value, yielding a living death. In short, love delivers life. Not simply biological continuance, but spiritually blessed life. Love delivers us to the living waters of life. Value, the meaningfulness of life, is created and sustained by love.

In this dynamic, rather than living over and against everything else — seeing salvation and security in the ability to dominate, living in a fundamentally conflicted relationship with all others, futilely attempting to value ourselves in utter isolation — we find value delivered on the far side of having been seized by love for all creatures of every kind. Now we are affirmed and filled with joy and delight because we do not live over and against all those who are other, but precisely in the light of having been seized by love for them. As I will now strive to unfold in detail, literally all spiritual value is delivered *through* having been seized by love for every creature, for people, other animals and plants, through having been seized indirectly but decisively by love for ourselves, and through delight in all the rest of creation.

5. Living Having Been Seized by Love for Ourselves: Living Gift

Let me be sure to make clear how in all of this I am speaking indirectly (as is necessary and appropriate) yet decidedly about the manifestation and affirmation not only of others but also of each of ourselves. The affirmation of ourselves in accord with the way of dominion contrasts decisively with the modern affirmation of self, which, from the Cartesian "I" to the

Heideggerian *Dasein* (with its ultimately self-centered concern), begins from the isolated "me" and thus inexorably wraps us up in the logic of domination.[7] By contrast, in accord with the way of dominion and the paradox of friendship and love, we first find ourselves affirmed in the light of having been seized by love for others.

We first find ourselves in relation to our love for others because that is where we are first manifest to ourselves as response-able and — already in the having been seized — as eternally beloved. As the Jewish philosopher Emmanuel Levinas says, the "imperative to love," which we interpret as the imperative of having been seized in and by love for another, "is also election and love reaching [the one] who is invested by it in [his or her] uniqueness qua responsible one."[8] That is, the imperative to love, the having been seized in and by love for others, is simultaneously the manifestation of a love in and by which I, too, am seized. (In Christian theology this is also referred to as my "election" by God.) Awakening to election is talked about in terms of salvation because I, too, am manifest as beloved when, in and through the having been seized, I am taken up and held in the transcending reality of the love. It is not only that we can see ourselves

---

7. Note that, according to the most precise late-twentieth-century secular understanding, every "subject" is a narrative fiction designating a significant locus from the view of one level of understanding/interpretation (e.g., the human), but ultimately what is thus designated a "subject" is a part of the flow within a mindless (i.e., largely deterministic, possibly partly indeterministic) flux. This is the perspective that Richard Dawkins reflects (though it is unclear whether he has fully grasped the philosophical implications of his contentions) in his notorious but, given the mainstream of modern Western understanding, wholly consistent contention that the decisive evolutionary unit is not any individual creature but the replicators that use groups of creatures to replicate themselves. These replicators "swarm in huge colonies, safe inside gigantic lumbering robots, sealed off from the outside world, communicating with it by tortuous indirect routes, manipulating it by remote control. They are in you and in me; they created us, body and mind; and their preservation is the ultimate rationale for our existence. They have come a long way, these replicators. Now they go by the name of genes, and we are their survival machines" (*The Selfish Gene* [Oxford: Oxford University Press, 1999], pp. 19-20). Note that the "selfish" in Dawkins's title is not ethical in the classic sense. It only describes certain blind tendencies that describe characteristic behavior of some survival machines as they "beat out" others in the "struggle" for existence.

8. Emmanuel Levinas, *Of God Who Comes to Mind*, trans. Bettina Bergo (Stanford: Stanford University Press, 1986), p. ix.

as beloved in and through the gaze of others who are seized by love for us. Even when we have been seized by love for our enemies, who are not awakened to love for us, we ourselves are nonetheless taken up in love, and we live in the light of having been seized by love.

In other words, we are not delivered through others' love for us. The gift of love is the gift of God, who is love. The gift does not come from any other creatures. We are held by the love that comes to us for other creatures (the flowers of the field, every sparrow, every child). That is why, to the degree that we live shut off from love for others, that is, to the degree we live the logic of domination, we live proportionally closed off from love for ourselves (or, on the contrary, that is why we know ourselves as forgiven as we also forgive).[9]

6. The "Tower of Babel"

I am suggesting that, with regard to affirmation of our own selves, it is not a matter of self-affirmation, self-assertion, self-grounding, or claims to intrinsic value, or a basic right, but of one's having been seized in and by love. Accordingly, the seven-days narrative does not affirm any creatures or even God insofar as they live over and against everything else. It does not see salvation and security in the ability to dominate. The seven-days narrative does not affirm or even begin to describe creatures or Creator living in fundamentally conflicted relationships. To the contrary, the having been seized by love is proclaimed to reveal and to be the primordial and ultimate reality.

At the far end of the narrative arc of the primeval history, at the heart of the closing "Tower of Babel" narrative, one discovers a people intent on self-affirmation, self-assertion, self-grounding. The narrative turns upon the people's determination to build a brick city and tower so that they might make a name for themselves and so that they might protect themselves from being defeated and scattered abroad, and thereby rendered frightfully vulnerable in the war of all against all: "Come, let us build ourselves a [brick] city, and a tower with its top in the heavens, and let us

9. Thus, for instance, the first step in the *via negativa* is purgation.

make a name for ourselves; otherwise we shall be scattered abroad upon the face of the whole earth" (Gen. 11:4, NRSV).

In brief, the ancient people of Babel are motivated by the spiritually death-dealing logic of domination. When it appears that the people may be successful in their tragic pursuit, God intervenes to at least forestall spiritual disaster by scattering them into diverse language groups. The primeval history ends on this ambiguous and sobering real-world note. And in this context, the more profound spiritual meaning of what most likely started out as an origin-of-diverse-languages narrative becomes manifest.

The contrast between the logic of domination and the way of dominion and the proclamation of the grace of God, that is, the proclamation that love is primordial and ultimate, is delineated fully and profoundly in the Flood and seven-days-of-Creation narratives. But the primeval history is utterly realistic, and so by the close of the primeval history the human heart, evil from youth, is still striving to establish itself within the cosmos by building an impressive city and tower. Put in proper perspective (e.g., by contrast with the scale of the Ancient Near East, let alone with the scale of planet earth or the galaxy), the plain absurdity of all such attempts to dominate reality is patent. Nonetheless, such attempts continue across cultures and history to our day. That is, the logic of domination is not in retreat, to put it mildly.

Immediately after the Tower of Babel narrative, the primeval history, which opens with the narrative of the seven days of Creation, closes with a final genealogy. And as we have already discussed, the next narrative after that in the book of Genesis, the narrative that marks the transition from the primeval history to the narrative of the nation of Israel, moves directly to the call of Abram. The contrast between the call of Abram and the Tower of Babel narrative is striking. I will cite the critical transition verse once again:

> Now the Lord said to Abram, "Go from your country and your kindred and your father's house to the land that I will show you. I will make of you a great nation, and I will bless you, and make your name great, so that you will be a blessing. I will bless those who bless you, and the one who curses you I will curse; and in you all the families of the earth shall be blessed." (Gen. 12:1-3)

Follow me, God says, and I will make your name great, and I will make of you a great nation. I will bless you and through you all families of the earth — all those families that came out of the ark? — will be blessed. In the wake of the primeval history, it is clear that what it is to follow God, to be great, to be a great nation, a *good and faithful* nation, and to be a blessing to all, comes, whether for individuals or for peoples, not through self-assertion or self-affirmation, not in accord with the logic of domination, but in the true spirit of Godly dominion.

In marked contrast to the internally grounded, self-initiative of Noah, who attempts to decide and dictate to God the nature of the covenant, the narrative of the call of Abram emphasizes the initial passivity of Abram, the initiative of God, and then the faithful response of Abram in responding to God. That is, what is portrayed is not the decisive initiative of Abram, not Abram making a decision to act in and out of himself as he creates his own identity, but Abram's faithful response to having been seized by love for all others. (Let's be sure to note that as the ever-realistic Genesis narrative progresses, it becomes clear that Abram, like the rest of us, surely and repeatedly fails to remain faithful.) But the narrative also makes clear that the saving, the having-been-seized-by-love, remains constant. (In theological terms: God is righteous and faithful, God is gracious, God's love is eternal, from everlasting to everlasting.)

What follows in the balance of Genesis, the rest of the Pentateuch, and in the historical writings of the Jewish Scriptures and the Christian Old Testament, is a brutally and admirably honest theology of the checkered history of the ancient Israelites, a story of the history of Israel that in part is written with the theological objective of praising and commending individuals and peoples who lived the way of dominion while naming and proclaiming hard truths to and/or about those who succumbed to the logic of domination (e.g., this is how we would read what scholars call the "Deuteronomic history").[10]

Therefore, when the primeval history closes its narrative arc with the Tower of Babel narrative, it realistically returns us to our real, historical world, a world in which people strive to establish themselves in accord with

10. Remember that much of the material in Gen. 12–50 predates our received version of the primeval history (i.e., Gen. 1–11).

the logic of domination. But now the futility of what those who are hostage to the logic of domination consider to be success is apparent. The saving opportunity opened up by defeat and hopelessness (i.e., regarding our own exertion of power) is also apparent. The vision of an alternative and true way (always already available and wonderful) has been proclaimed.

In summary, the significance, acuity, and spiritual genius of the primeval history's proclamation that the way of God is the way of dominion is now apparent. In the light of the way of dominion, one is affirmed and filled with joy and delight because one does not live over against all those who are other, but precisely through having been seized by love for them. That is, value, meaningfulness, joy, communion, *koinonia* — ourselves as precious, response-able, and beloved — all are delivered *through* our having been seized by love for all the innumerable other creatures that fill every nook and cranny of our enchanted world (the more the richer!). The primeval history clearly understands and proclaims that dominion and love yield life, value, meaningfulness, joy, and *koinonia*.

By contrast, as is now clear, domination lives and yields death. In stark contrast to the predominant modern Western mode of self-assertion, the primeval history proclaims that we receive ourselves as loving and beloved wholly as gift, not through the assertion of intrinsic value or assertion of inalienable rights, nor as the product of self-affirmation, let alone through what many twenty-first-century theorists refer to as "pure violence" (sheer assertion and political establishment of power over who will live and die, the decisive consideration for an influential trajectory of neo-Hobbesian political theory). In short, love, or agape, a love that precedes and seizes us if we do not harden our hearts; a love that continually seeks to awaken us; a supra-naturalistic love — this love delivers us, here and now, into a transcending life that is primordially and ultimately a life of communion, affirmation, joy, and delight, into the life of faith and life eternal (even if still mortal).

7. The Pain of Awakening

Let me digress momentarily in order to acknowledge explicitly that awakening will bring not only joy but also pain in a world filled with suffering and injustice. The pain will only be amplified when we are caught in situations where the calls of various creatures are in irremediable conflict. This was an awareness all too clear to Albert Schweitzer, whose principle of "reverence for life" and distinctive understanding of the "ethical" corresponds to the spirit of the seven-days narrative. One is "ethical," Schweitzer insists, to the degree that one

> refrains from afflicting injury upon anything that lives. . . . Life as such is holy. . . . When working by candlelight on a summer night, one would rather keep the windows closed and breathe stuffy air than see insect after insect fall on the table with wings that are singed. If one walks along the street after rain and notices an earthworm which has lost its way . . . one carries it from the death-dealing stones to the grass. . . . One is not afraid of being smiled at as a sentimentalist.[11]

Schweitzer, however, lived in the real world. He regularly killed insects and viruses and other animals to protect patients in his missionary hospital in Africa. Schweitzer never killed casually or for luxury, but only when it was necessary. And he never killed with an easy heart, never considered it his right as a superior creature, but only as lamentable and evil necessity in a fallen world.

Schweitzer, then, knew full well how spiritual sensitivity to every creature could become a searing sensitivity in a world full of suffering and injustice, and in a world in which the life-needs of the various creatures are in irremediable conflict. So Schweitzer took care to specify that for the person who truly lives a life full of love and concern for all creatures, life will "become harder . . . in every respect than it would be if one lived for oneself, but at the same time it will be richer, more beautiful, and happier. It will become, instead of mere living, a real experience of life."[12] In

---

11. Albert Schweitzer, *Kultur und Ethik* (München: C. H. Beck, 1960), pp. 331-32, as translated by G. W. Bromiley and T. F. Torrance in Karl Barth, *Church Dogmatics* III/4 (Edinburgh: T&T Clark, 1961), p. 349. Renowned twentieth-century theologian Karl Barth, who is typically and correctly criticized for his strong tendency to focus only on God and humans, nonetheless cited these very words and said, "Those who can only smile at this point are themselves subjects for tears" (*Church Dogmatics,* III/4, p. 349).

12. Albert Schweitzer, *Out of My Life and Thought* (New York: Henry Holt, 1933), p. 268.

other words, instead of living death, one will live life. This is quite simply the most honest and authentic spiritual stance possible for moral people, that is, for people who have been seized by love for all the creatures that surround and summon them, no matter how painful.

In raising pigs for slaughter, Mr. Burge, that loving old pig farmer, did exercise domination. We do not live in paradise. In a world in which the essential life-needs of various creatures conflict and the relative weight of the calls of various creatures must be adjudicated, at certain points and to some degree, we need to live the logic of domination. But Mr. Burge apparently also strove to maximize dominion in his love and care for his animals, and he thereby enriched the value and joy of their lives and of his life — though again, only to the degree that he did not love others in order to enrich the value of his life. His love of his pigs no doubt increased his pain at their slaughter.

In that National Public Radio story, McChesney also spoke to the manager of a factory "farm." The man was not a monster; rather, he was the manager of a factory concerned with "production units" and maximizing production. He did not have any interest in naming the nearly 25,000 "units" he processed a year, let alone in loving them. Given the suffering and death he was responsible for inflicting, this hardening of his heart, this closing of his spiritual eyes to all those creatures, may have protected him — superficially at least — from significant pain.

But it is crucial for that factory manager and for us to realize that he was also a victim. The life he led processing units as a manager in a factory was not nearly as rich, beautiful, happy, or tragic as Mr. Burge's life as a pig farmer living among pigs. To the degree that the farm manager mechanized the animals and the "farm," he mechanized himself. To the degree that he needed to see all animals, let alone all plants, as machines, he alienated himself from all creatures and drained his world of value, for he emptied his world of love, beauty, communion, and joy. The real threat for this man, the spiritual threat, is that to the degree he became factory-efficient and superficially shielded himself from exposure to significant pain by mechanizing all those creatures — to precisely that same degree he became less alive. For to precisely the degree that he hardened his heart to having been seized by love for each one of those pigs, he diminished the richness of his world, lost the indirect affirmation of love for himself as a fellow creature, became the inhabitant of a sorely diminished world, and lived a living death.

In the same way, given the modern Western tendency to relate to all other creatures and all the rest of creation in terms of domination, the threat to modern Western humans is that we will increasingly see and treat the whole world, even other creatures, as machines, that we will increasingly render the whole world into a factory and thus unwittingly dehumanize, diminish, and devalue all of life, that we will increasingly make machines of ourselves, make a machine of life, that we will unintentionally but effectively find ourselves living death instead of living life.

Even scientists who reject belief in God and see the seven-days-of-Creation narrative as backward replicate the dynamics I am critiquing here when they struggle to ground human dignity and worth in some capacity that clearly sets humans apart from other creatures. We do not enrich our lives and lift ourselves up by diminishing the value of other creatures. Clearly, humans are at the top of the hierarchy of creatures in terms of intelligence, language, and culture. But we do not establish value by affirming these distinctions from the rest of creation and then in their light devaluing all that is, in terms of this hierarchy, beneath us.

We are a part of the hierarchy along with everything else. We are "humans from humus," creatures among creatures in creation. Moreover, in accord with this reading of Genesis, even God, by virtue of creating, becomes inextricably connected to this hierarchy. Our value is not intrinsic; it is relative — relative to the rest of the hierarchy (a critique of the standard modern understanding of "intrinsic value" is implicit here). All the hierarchy rises and falls together. For us to affirm our worth by emphasizing our superiority to what we devalue as worthless is, Looney Tunes style, to saw off the limb to which we are clinging.

Of course, from the materialist perspective, where one affirms reality only insofar as it is empirical, where to be rational is by definition to act in one's own interests, there is no better court of appeal. Looney Tunes it is and ever must be. That is why the solipsistic modern "self" from Descartes to Heidegger (you alone live toward and die your own death), a "self" that must establish and justify itself ex nihilo (i.e., "from nothing"), becomes predominant in mainstream modern Western thought, and that is why this modern understanding of "self" and "reality" inevitably engenders the specters of anomie and nihilism. Indeed, that is why anomie and nihilism have quite understandably and inevitably plagued modern Western thought.

The seven-days-of-Creation narrative avoids these perils by affirming the value-creating dynamics of agape. It does this by proclaiming God's dominion over creation and calling us to a similar dominion. The narrative does not issue this "call" as a command, but it strives to awaken us by painting an inspiring, wondrous, beautiful vision of a perfectly perfect world in which all creatures live blessed, peaceful, and joyful lives. With this picture, the seven-days-of-Creation narrative strives to awaken us to the infinite value of every creature (day after day, the refrain: "It was good," "it was good"). There is no hierarchy of value or worth because the narrative is striving to awaken us to the infinite worth of every creature in a world full of all kinds of creatures. The breadth of the affirmation is intended to enchant the whole world and awaken us to having been seized by love for all the creatures that surround us in this enchanted world.

Many people, for instance, have been awakened by love for a tree and have found themselves embraced in its comfort, its fortitude, its life. More mysteriously, trees participate in an elemental way of being that we enjoy as well. And communion with trees can help us realize ways of being more fully — and help us inhabit them more elementally. There is a communion and peace that inhabits us when we take time in the middle of a forest, when we learn from a tree, when we open ourselves to love of a tree. This is a communion that is not available when, for instance, we are sitting in the middle of even a very quiet parking lot surrounded by cars, or when we are sitting in the middle of a forest and obliterating it with the mental filter "board feet" (as in "board feet" of lumber).

Again, it is sometimes necessary and appropriate to see board feet of lumber — though even then, just as with the far more painful case of Pug (e.g., the slices of Pug on the deli sandwich), there should always be a stinging sense of painful compromise: Do we really need that ham sandwich? But those who see only board feet, production units, or slices of ham — those who close themselves off from love for all these wonderful creatures — those unfortunate people, sadly, are lost and shut off from the love that would seize them, shut off from their own response-ability, shut off from indirectly having been seized by a saving, gracious love for themselves, and shut off from the joy of the transcending communion into which we are caught up when we are seized by love for a creature who is simultaneously seized by love for us. To be cut off in these ways from other creatures and from ourselves is to suffer a horrible spiritual loss.

The seven-days narrative avoids the devastating perils of the logic of domination and strives to awaken us by testifying to dominion. It affirms and seeks to awaken us to the value-affirming, value-sustaining, life-giving dynamics of friendship and love. It tries to awaken those who are living death by means of an impossibly beautiful vision of a wholly peaceable and blessed world. It tries to awaken them by describing and thereby proclaiming God's dominion over creation. Through its portrayal of God's delight and joy in every creature, the narrative hopes and strives to awaken us to divine inspiration, to the transcending communion of having been seized by love for every creature, to a life of loving, saved and saving, life-giving dominion.

At the heart of this way of affirming and sustaining value lies awakening — not establishing, proving, founding, or creating — but awakening to a reality by which we have been seized, or, if we allow our hearts and minds to be opened, by which we will be seized. We are not called to make a decision or to follow a command. Rather, the beautiful vision of the peaceable creation is meant to rouse us from our slumber, to awaken us to having been seized in and by love. To the degree that we awaken, we will live in the light of having been seized by love for all creatures, and to that degree we will live the way of dominion, we will act and move and receive our be-ing, as the gift of primordial and ultimate love, that is, as the gift of God — alpha and omega. In other words, we will live in the light of having been seized in and by love, which is to say, we will live by faith that is the gift of grace.

CHAPTER EIGHT

A Knowing Idealism

The Decisive Asymmetry

1. Naïve Idealism?

The vision of a wholly peaceable and blessed world is beautiful and inspiring. But is it not *far too* beautiful and thus deceptively — even dangerously — inspiring? Even if the seven-days narrative is not doing science, must it not still be faulted for getting real-world moral and creaturely reality wrong? Isn't any sober reader forced to conclude that the vision of the seven-days narrative, no matter how wonderful, is naïve and unrealistic? Isn't it even potentially dangerous insofar as it tempts us toward a highly vulnerable idealism that is bound to be continually disappointed?

Even some theologians have in recent decades characterized the idealistic seven-days and Edenic portion of the Adam-and-Eve Creation narratives as childish, and have interpreted the disobedience of Adam and Eve and their exit from the Garden of Eden as an affirmation of humans coming of age, taking responsibility (in the modern sense of asserting autonomy), and recognizing the intractably merciless ways of the real world. This reading exactly reverses the classic interpretation of the Adam-and-Eve narrative's depiction of the Fall. In classic understanding, Adam and Eve's expulsion from the Garden is a cautionary tale about the character and consequences of the attempt to make oneself the autonomous measure of all things.[1] But again, today some see the spirit, faith, and testimony of

---

1. I cannot begin to explore this incredibly complex narrative. Suffice it to say that

the seven-days narrative as childish foolishness. By contrast, those who "face up" to the Hobbesian/Darwinian "truth" revealed by modern philosophy and science in an age of "reason" and "enlightenment" are thought to be truly adult.

In fact, predominant modern Western creation narratives (cosmologies) at best fail to take account of the moral realities that constitute the most profound dimension of our lives. At worst, they aid and abet immorality, for they fail to acknowledge, are generally incapable of discerning, and in significant ways obstruct our having been seized by love for all creatures. I have in mind here the materialism of Hobbes (the ultimacy of enlightened selfishness), Descartes (the priority of "I thinking"), Nietzsche (transvaluation of values; the "ethical" as a species of the aesthetic), naturalism (unqualified Darwinism as total theory), and the ultimate priority of "I passionate/concerned over myself and my own coming death" in the Heidegger of *Being and Time*. These quintessentially modern creation narratives are all variations on the Hobbesian/Darwinian cosmology. Because they are all fundamentally amoral, they get moral reality profoundly and utterly wrong.

Nevertheless, doesn't the seven-days-of-Creation narrative also get moral reality profoundly wrong? Doesn't our moral and ethical realism also require us to demur when confronted with the seven-days narrative's vision of a wholly peaceable world? That is, if we embrace moral and ethical realism and honestly acknowledge the character and possibilities of the world we live in, aren't we forced to conclude that the peaceable Creation vision also gets moral reality wrong — in that it fails to acknowledge moral and creaturely reality's ambiguous character? Indeed, doesn't the Enuma Elish — which affirms the reality of the moral while remaining realistic about the morally ambiguous character of our world and its potentials — now emerge as more realistic than either the amoral modern Western creation narratives or the peaceable world fantasies of Isaiah and the seven days of Creation?

To review, the Enuma Elish proclaims that reality is, ultimately, mor-

---

I would interpret "eating from the tree of knowledge of good and evil" in relation to the dynamics of a step from dominion to domination and also, in terms defined below, in relation to the move from the pure moral to the moral plus the ethical.

ally ambiguous (Apsu and Tiamat), but that a relatively pure idea of the good can be carved out (Marduk, made out of the pure interior of Apsu). It contends that we humans are not pure (we are made out of Tiamat's consort, Qingu), but urges that if we order ourselves in accord with the good (Marduk and his precepts), we can establish a social realm of relative order and good (as Marduk established an ordered realm via the defeat of Tiamat). We must remain ever vigilant, however, because the hard-won realm of relative order and good is forever threatened by chaotic forces lurking both within (we are made of Qingu) and without (the earthly realm is made up of Tiamat and, ultimately, all reality flows from Tiamat and Apsu).

In short, according to the Enuma Elish, relatively good agents manage through heroic effort to carve out a relatively good and ordered but continually threatened realm from an encompassing reality that is internally and externally morally chaotic and conflicted.[2] This certainly appears to be more realistic than either the modern Western creation narratives (inaccurately amoral) or the seven-days-of-Creation narrative (naïvely idealistic). While I remain impressed by the acute insight of the Enuma Elish, and while I admit that at first glance the seven-days-of-Creation narrative looks naïvely idealistic, I will argue that the primeval history of Genesis, including the radically idealistic vision of the seven-days narrative, provides a far more accurate, realistic, and sophisticated account of reality than does the Enuma Elish (let alone varieties of Hobbesian/ Darwinian materialism).

2. The Decisive Asymmetry: The "Yes" within every "No"

The seal was trapped in an industrial out-take tank on the coast of California. There was some sort of elevated boardwalk along the beach from which the tank could be seen, and soon someone spotted the seal and realized its plight. By the time news crews arrived, a rescue effort was underway. Guiding the seal back out to sea proved difficult. Workers struggled

---

2. There is no "pure violence" here, for the reality of the good is affirmed.

to help the increasingly desperate animal escape. As the hours passed, a large crowd of families — moms, dads, kids — gathered to cheer on the rescuers. Eventually, to the accompaniment of many smiles and happy cries, the rescuers managed to lead the seal through the correct passageways and free it into the open ocean. With fast bounds above the water surface and dives below it, the seal could be seen swimming excitedly out to sea. Perhaps seventy-five yards out — still within sight of the humans onshore — an orca banged up into view, slammed the seal into the air, caught it, and then submerged, the now limp seal hanging from its jaws.

While that sad ending is unusual, I take this to be a familiar "rescue" scenario. One routinely sees stories like this, usually with happy endings, on the local and national news. This is in itself heartening. On the whole, despite the betrayals of modern Western rationality and the condescending and dismissive attitude that many intellectuals tend to assume with such stories, the fact is that the vast majority of us are moved when we see a creature in distress. We value efforts to save creatures (including humans), and we feel joy when they are rescued or freed. The pictures of smiling children clapping gleefully only make us more aware of the restrained inner feelings that we more reserved adults have. And in this story, the tears of those same children at the fate of the seal are just as real, though this time perhaps the children truly were more genuinely uncomprehending than we adults are, whose hopes and expectations may well have been blunted through previous bitter experience.

Indeed, the bitterness of disappointed expectations can lead some to a gruff rejection of any initial feeling for the seal: better never to love and hope at all than to love and hope when some eventual bitter end is a foregone conclusion. Of course, that tragic but understandable reaction is anything but a rejection of the reality of our spiritual sensitivity. On the contrary, it speaks to unbearable sensitivity; it betrays unbearable pain.

The worry about the seal, the concern for its desperation, for its survival, the thankfulness for the efforts of the rescue workers, the joy in the seal's release, the joy at its joy, or — if the orca is what chased it into the shelter of the out-take tank in the first place — the anguish over its anguish, the pain at its despair, the sadness at its death and, from another perspective, the happiness for the orca, for its success in the hunt and in its struggle to survive — all of these spiritual responses in all their complexity and tension are real. Moreover, in all their real-world, vale-of-tears contradictions, these responses are the manifestation of the same love that is alpha and omega.

As such news stories illustrate, just as the story of the Flood (when all of the horrible violence and injustice is not evaded) heightens our spiritual sensitivities, thus do stories on the news about the suffering or deaths of other creatures (including humans) typically heighten spiritual sensitivities (such stories are typically followed by Web addresses where donations can be made to help survivors or prevent future tragedy). In this vale of tears, of course, most of us have grown accustomed to steeling ourselves, bracing ourselves against the harsh realities of life. The bitterness of disappointed expectations can lead us to the gruff hardening of our hearts: better never to love and hope at all, than to love and hope when some eventual bitter end is a foregone conclusion. If we have steeled ourselves in this way, then we will resist the apparently naïve, highly vulnerable, bound-to-be-disappointed idealism of the seven-days-of-Creation narrative.

It is crucial to realize, however, that this tragic but understandable reaction is anything but a rejection of the reality of our love for other creatures. To the contrary, it speaks to unbearable love and sensitivity. It betrays unbearable pain. For in the very act of steeling ourselves, in the very act of hardening our hearts, we betray to ourselves the truth of the pain we struggle to deny. For the act of steeling, while surely understandable, is a struggle to desensitize ourselves to other creatures that is itself motivated by profound aversion to the searing pain we feel precisely over the violation of their lives. The desire to steel ourselves, then, is rooted in the very reality we struggle to deny.

This struggle to steel ourselves is often cloaked in language of "growing up," "facing up," or "getting realistic." And the struggle can, unfortunately, be largely successful. But the struggle is, in fact, an exercise in self-deception. Indeed, since we are in reality moral beings, success in the struggle to eviscerate our response-ability is a form of self-inflicted spiritual mutilation.[3] To the degree that we have not succeeded in hardening

---

3. I believe that what I am asserting here is essentially continuous with Charles Taylor's depiction of the "mutilation" constituted by a Nietzschean eliding of the ethical

our hearts, not succeeded in steeling ourselves, not succeeded in desensitizing ourselves, deceiving ourselves, *wounding* ourselves, we ache for that seal, for its confusion, pain, and loss. At the same time, and for precisely the same reasons (i.e., our having been seized by love for all other creatures), we are joyful for the orca. We name and own our having been seized by love for both creatures: no denial, no gruff rejection, no hardening of our hearts. We face the unresolvable contradiction squarely. We call our world fallen. We are as realistic as the Flood narrative about the world in which we live.

So imagine a world in which all of the searing sensitivity to suffering, loss, or disappointment afflicting any and all creatures is not in any way denied but is instead wholly owned. And in the face of that full-bodied owning of our anguish over the violation of other creatures, imagine that we recognizes the "yes," our absolutely sure convictions concerning how creatures *should* flourish and be joyful, a conviction that is presumed by and breathes fire into that impassioned "no." Imagine that we discern the significance of that decisive asymmetry, the absolute priority of the "yes," the realization that every "no" is at heart "yes-violated."

This is to realize that the love by which we have been seized is primordial and ultimate. This is to realize that, far from being overcome by evil, this love lies at the heart of every recognition of evil as such. It is to realize that, far from being overcome by intense evil, this love is all the more intensely manifest in the face of intense evil. Taken up in wonder about the realization that love is not defeated but revealed in the heart of our screamed "no!" we can realistically imagine ourselves (if leisure for reflection comes again) owning and proclaiming that that "yes," that love that sees evil as such, that love that would have it otherwise, is primordial and ultimate, alpha and omega, divine.

In other words, we can imagine ourselves beginning with the Flood narrative, an utterly realistic narrative in which the most horrific eventualities are imagined, in which the intractability of earthly strife and human culpability ("hearts evil from youth") is acknowledged, and yet a narrative where, precisely when one might be most tempted to respond with anger,

---

for the sake of self-affirmation. See Taylor, *Sources of the Self: The Making of the Modern Identity* (Cambridge, MA: Harvard University Press, 1989), pp. 447-55, 515-21.

vengeance, and violence, or to imagine the gods angry and demanding violent recompense (e.g., bloody, tit-for-tat sacrifice), precisely in the midst of the horror — precisely when screaming the most intense "no" — one recognizes instead, at the heart of the passion of the "no," the having-been-seized-by-love for all others.

Precisely where one might expect anger, one instead discovers the love that is of another order and not defeated, a love that does not respond in kind, that has no interest in returning evil for evil, that has no interest in vengeance and violence in return for evil and violence, that is not vulnerable to evil's antispiritual venom. The "no" is not silenced, evil is not denied, resistance and attempts to bring aid and relief remain urgent, our pain and lament endure — and, in extremis, may be psychologically debilitating (see below) — but the priority and resilience of the "yes" still shines forth at the heart of every "no."

As we are taken up in wonder by the transcending reality of the "yes," we can sense the character and power of the spirit that inspired the rainbow covenant, the spirit that inspired the proclamation that love is divine, that God is love, the spirit that inspired the proclamation that love is of another order, that love transcends tit-for-tat, eye-for-an-eye economies of justice, that gracious love reigns over all. One will feel the character and power of the spirit to which the redactors of the primeval history hope to awaken us, a spirit that is not at all naïve or deceived about the character of our world, the spirit of the impassioned "no" to suffering and evil, the spirit of a gracious love, of the transcending "yes" of affirmation, and a spirit that defiantly refuses to let the intractable realities of life in this fallen world force denial of the equally real and transcending power of our most profound, sure, and cherished having-been-seized-by-love for all the wonderful host of creatures.

In the light of the recognition of the asymmetry, one can imagine wanting to cast the discrete contours of the transcending "yes" into brilliant relief by giving it utterly unambiguous, visible form, and so of painting a picture not only of the fallen, strife-ridden, hurting, unjust world we know all too well (e.g., the Flood narrative, including its pre- and post-Flood descriptions of the state of the world), but also by painting the picture of a world imagined as it would be if it were wholly ordered by gracious love, a world that is only "yes," a world where no "no" (no "yes-violated") ever arises, a world without any evil, a world in which all live wholly blessed lives in perfect harmony, a world where animals feast only on seeds and fruits, where the leopard lies with the baby goat, where the lion eats straw, where the child, the rattlesnake, the rat, and the cobra play together, where there is no harm, no injustice, no want, no disappointment, no mourning, no pain, no suffering *anywhere* — for awakening to having been seized by love for every creature covers the earth like the waters cover the sea. One can imagine painting the picture of a perfectly perfect realm; one can imagine painting the pictures of the seven days of Creation and of the eschatological narratives of Isaiah.

3. A Perfectly Perfect Realm?
Moral, Aesthetic, and Ethical Good

It is not uncommon to hear people object that the idea of a world without any evil is not only unrealistic, given the evil suffusing our world, but that it is literally unthinkable because "evil" and "good" are mutually codependent concepts. That is, like the mutually codependent concepts east and west, evil and good literally cannot be thought of one without the other. Thus the idea of a world that is perfectly perfect, only good, utterly lacking in evil, is literally incoherent.

In response to this confused contention, which sounds reasonable enough at first blush, I need to add some precision to our understanding of good and evil by distinguishing among moral, aesthetic, and ethical good. Let me begin with the observation that conventional English is philosophically profound insofar as in English we do not speak about a violation of evil, but only about a violation of the good. We do not speak of a violation of evil, because evil cannot be violated. Evil cannot be violated because evil itself is fundamentally a violation, the violation of some creature (i.e., yes-violated).

Even in common speech, then, evil presumes a fall from what is, in principle (though not in history), a supraethical realm where we live in perfect love and harmony, apart from any evil. Therefore, "evil" correlates to the ethical realm proper, where one encounters evil, and good in contrast to evil. This means, as commonly observed, that evil, good in the ethical sense (i.e., good in contrast to evil), ethics and the ethical realm proper — all these do indeed arise simultaneously with the violation of creatures and are indeed mutually codependent concepts (i.e., they dependently co-originate).

It does not follow, however, that if one is to have good in *any* sense that one must have evil, for we can distinguish two senses of good that are meaningful in the absence of any evil. First, there is good in the sense of the transcending joy of having been seized by love for others, that is, what we will call good in a *moral* sense ("moral" because it is other-responsive, but not yet "ethical" because there is no yes-violated). I do not need any concept of evil in order to enjoy and conceive of the good of having been seized by love for others (agape). Second, there is good in the sense of delight (i.e., love in the sense of eros) in some creature or thing, for instance, in a symphony, a rainbow, a fresh-picked bowl of strawberries, or the body of a lover — that is, good in an *aesthetic* sense. And again, there is good in a familiar sense that has already been mentioned: the sense in which we judge resistance to injustice or suffering to be good, good in contrast to evil, good in contrast to "yes-violated," good in an *ethical* sense.

It is simplistic, then, to see "good" and "evil" as wholly codependent, for only the ethical sense of good is mutually codependent with evil. A perfectly perfect realm, full of moral and aesthetic good, full of agape and eros, and devoid of even the concept of evil, is entirely thinkable. That is why what one usually and more reasonably hears in objection to the vision of the perfectly peaceable creation portrayed in the seven-days-of-Creation narrative is that it is unrealistic, childish. One does not usually hear the objection that the perfectly peaceable world of the seven-days narrative literally cannot be thought.

4. The Decisive Asymmetry:
The Substantial Priority of the Good

The asymmetry between good and evil makes clear that, since evil is a violation of a creature, it has no independent existence. Evil's status is wholly derivative; it is substantially (if not historically/temporally) dependent on good in the *moral* sense, for "evil" arises only with the violation of a creature. Therefore, while *ethical* good does dependently co-originate with evil, *moral* good, the good of the call of having been seized in and by love, is independent and not only conceptually but substantially (if not historically) prior to — and autonomous from — evil. Even the most intense experience of evil, the screamed "no!" — and I do not deny the reality of the violation, which may utterly consume others and/or us — already depends conceptually and substantially on moral good. Recognition of this derivative status of evil has led theologians to speak of evil as a privation of the good (i.e., a violation of the good, of the good that *should* obtain for some creatures), as a pure absence, or as a form of nothingness.

In some cases moral and aesthetic kinds of good may be intimately related. For instance, though I cannot go into detail here, one may delight (aesthetic good) in the physical body of a lover. Obviously, insofar as one's lover is a creature — in contrast to a symphony or a rainbow — delight in the lover's body should be conjoined with a having been seized by love for one's lover (moral good), else the delight in the body becomes unethical. That is, "delight" becomes a violation of another insofar as one possesses the other as an object of delight while one hardens one's heart to having been seized by love for that other. Depending on the circumstances, the severity of the violation can range from mild (two single adults engaging in a mutually agreed-on and solely self-interested one-night stand) to heinous (rape). This is also the character of the violation when one delights in a ham sandwich while wholly forgetting Pug.

Neither do we in English speak of a violation of the aesthetic (e.g., a violation of beauty). But the reason we do not speak of a violation of beauty is critically different from the reason we do not speak about a violation of evil. We do not speak about a violation of beauty because aesthetic good is rooted not in response to creatures but in the delight creatures take in other creatures or things (e.g., a rainbow). So, with regard to aesthetic delight, no "violation" is possible, for there is nothing involved that is a possible subject of moral violation. Of course, some symphonies or paintings may be utterly lacking in accomplishment, an awful waste of time and even unpleasant to experience; but insofar as they are wholly aesthetic works or objects, that is, insofar as engaging or consuming them does not violate any other, they can only be "bad," or "violations," in a nonmoral and thus nonethical sense (e.g., "a violation of good taste").

This is not to say that what purports or was intended to be aesthetic cannot cross over into ethical territory. But at the point of crossing over, that is, at the point at which the aesthetic work or object violates some creature, it manifests an ethical dimension, and so to that degree it ceases to be aesthetic and becomes ethical and subject to ethical criticism. Of course, there will be debate in numerous cases over where precisely to draw the line between the aesthetic and the ethical. But uncertainty over ethical boundaries is unsurprising and in no way undercuts our confidence in the overwhelming number of nonborderline cases.

Finally, moral good has priority over aesthetic good, for we are given to ourselves as beloved only in the light of having been seized by love for all other creatures. Insofar as we are seized by love, we will never be able to delight in anything that involves the violation of the well-being of another creature. Aesthetic delight, then, is only possible for those who are awakened where there is no ethical violation. So the ethical has priority over the aesthetic.

This explains why violation of the moral, which marks the fall from the moral into the ethical, simply voids the possibility of any competing appeal to the aesthetic — as if a moral creature could delight in something that involves the violation of any other creature. There is, then, validity to the idea of "art for the sake of art" or, more precisely, "art for the sake of sheer delight," for delight does not have moral or ethical purpose. But the aesthetic is not possible if it in any way trades on the violation of any creature. So "art for the sake of art" is never a defense if any creature is violated, for then we are dealing not with the aesthetic dimension but with the ethical.[4] In short, evil is the violation of the well-

---

4. Note that, according to my account, the aesthetic is a species of the good, not vice versa (as is the case in modern thought where the category of the "moral" is a species of the aesthetic, that is, a species of what we desire, as in Hobbes). The aesthetic identifies that sphere of personally pleasing eventualities/possibilities within a realm where there is delightful variety in the absence of evil. As will become evident, this opens up a conceptual path to the transcending of the good/evil dichotomy that does not involve any Nietzschean "self-overcoming," materialist reduction, or any other denial of the reality of evil.

being of any creature. If those who are awakened are repulsed by evil, they will not see, in the same event, beauty. Evil will never be seen as beautiful for any who are morally awake (i.e., live in the light of having been seized by love).

In sum, a perfectly perfect realm — that is, a realm full of moral and aesthetic good and so wholly perfect that there is no space even for the idea of evil or good in the ethical sense — is thinkable. Moreover, there is a decisive asymmetry, for moral and aesthetic good are substantially (though not historically) prior to and independent of evil and good in the ethical sense. In contrast to moral and aesthetic good, evil and good in the ethical sense are derivative realities, for both depend on the violation of good in the moral sense.

5. The Perfectly Perfect Realm of the Seven-Days Narrative

As I detailed in my reflections on the Flood and the rainbow covenant, the final authors/redactors of the Flood and Creation narratives opened themselves utterly to every creature around them. They acknowledged every creature's pain and — precisely out of that highly refined level of sensitivity to all — realized that they had been seized by a love for every creature, by a love beyond tit-for-tat economies of justice. And thus they also affirmed that what is primordial and ultimate is a love that is beyond every eye-for-an-eye economy of justice, a love that is gracious. And they portrayed this primordial spiritual revelation, this birth of the recognition that love is divine, in the most momentous terms imaginable, in terms of a fundamental transformation in the very being of God, in terms of the birth of the God of grace.

Now when we who are awakened, that is, we who live in the wake of having been seized by love for all creatures, we who live with searing sensitivity to and in protest against all the pain, suffering, and injustice suffusing our world, when we who are awakened imagine the world that we would have, we quite naturally imagine a perfect world, a world with utterly no pain, no suffering, no injustice, no evil. Thanks to the prime-val history, we realize that if we are quite subtle, we will imagine a world utterly and wholly good in the moral and aesthetic senses but not good in the ethical sense, for a world utterly devoid of evil would also be devoid of good in the ethical sense. The redactors of the primeval history manifested and provoked just such philosophical subtlety, for they generated just such a vision of a perfectly perfect world.

As is commonly noted by commentators, the Hebrew term translated "good" in the seven-days narrative ("God saw that everything was good . . .") is not an ethical term. It is best understood in the sense of "wonderful" (with both moral and aesthetic dimensions), and does not signal ethical judgment or dispassionate evaluation; rather, it signals joy and delight, for example, when one turns and is swept up in a beautiful sunset (aesthetic delight) or when one is seized by love for a playing child (moral joy). Nor is the watery chaos over which the spirit of God initially hovers ascribed any ethical properties. Indeed, there are no ethical terms or categories in the seven-days-of-Creation narrative.

The seven-days narrative paints a picture of the spirit of God moving over a watery chaos: "The earth was without form *[tohu]* and void, and darkness was upon the face of the deep *[tehom]*; and the Spirit of God was moving over the face of the waters" (Gen. 1:2). The linguistic roots of *tohu* (i.e., formless) and of *tehom* (deep) are both similar to the root of *tiamat* (sea) and are very likely etymologically linked. This rightly brings to mind the Enuma Elish, for Marduk creates the world out of Tiamat after vanquishing her in a mighty battle.

But in stark contrast to the Enuma Elish narrative, the chaos in Genesis is not personified and it is not characterized as either good or evil. Chaos is by definition incompatible with the kind of ordered creation necessary for life to flourish. So chaos does threaten all creatures. But the watery chaos constitutes a nonethical threat: it is neither good nor evil. It is without intention, without end, and without personality. It simply is. Therefore, whereas Marduk must defeat the terrifying Tiamat, nothing opposes God. There is no struggle between God and other gods, nor is there any struggle between God and the watery chaos (i.e., the formless and void earth, the deep, the waters). To the contrary, day after day God simply speaks and chaos is progressively subdued and transformed into delightful places (days one through three), soon to be filled with creatures (days three through six), all of whom live in perfectly perfect harmony in a wholly peaceable creation.

As is now clear, there are no ethical terms or categories in the seven-days narrative because with profound philosophical subtlety it depicts a pure realm that is utterly separated from evil and good in the ethical sense (i.e., in the sense of "good in contrast to evil"). The peaceable creation is not "good" in an ethical sense because it is perfectly good, good apart from any evil, morally and aesthetically good. The concept of "good" in the ethical sense is not even thinkable within the bounds of the peaceable creation of the seven-days narrative. Thus the peaceable creation is "good" in the wholly moral and aesthetic senses of being without exception *wonderful:* a joyful (moral, think agape) and delightful (aesthetic, think eros) world filled with happy creatures who (1) all share, each in accord with its kind, in the transcending joy of having been seized by love for every other creature; (2) all see all others likewise seized by love for them; and (3) all delight, each in accord with its kind, in other creatures (e.g., the bodies of lovers) and inanimate creation (e.g., sun, rain, rainbows, stars).

The peaceable world is imagined as a place of creative and aesthetic diversity. The narrative portrays God as a loving artist, creating a wholly delightful world, a world full of diverse creative beings with aesthetically diverse tastes. Within a purely moral and aesthetic realm one can imagine a diversity of tastes and preferences even among creatures of the same kind (e.g., you like raspberries, I prefer strawberries; you like Haydn, I prefer Bach). So there is ample space in the peaceable creation for creatures to exercise free will and realize diverse creative potentials. Just as in a world without any evil one can imagine God freely choosing among and realizing diverse delightful possibilities, one can imagine humans and other creatures enjoying the freedom to choose among and realize diverse delights.

Freedom in the absence of evil, then, allows for free will and creativity in the ordinary senses (i.e., in philosophy's "libertarian" sense). Freedom in the absence of evil means only that the choices and diversity exist within a sphere in which every imagined and desired choice produces joy, happiness, and delight (or, at least, is not in any way evil or generating evil).[5]

---

5. This, by the way, would be free will exercised within the boundaries of "freedom" in the sense of Saint Paul. Paul defines "freedom" not as the unrestricted ability

6. The Knowing Idealism of the
Seven-Days-of-Creation Narrative

In the seven-days narrative nothing rivals God. God speaks over the watery chaos, and it responds. There is no ethical opposition. By contrast, the Enuma Elish affirms the reality of the moral but still sees ultimate reality as at best an admixture of evil and good (i.e., Tiamat and Apsu, out of whose "pure interior" Marduk is created). Marduk is a good and pure god, but Marduk (i.e., pure goodness) is a passion within a larger reality that is morally ambiguous and continually threatening. What is ultimate in the Enuma Elish is the duality of good/evil. The Enuma Elish affirms moral and ethical reality but does not recognize or theorize the decisive asymmetry, so it does not see the good (Marduk) as ultimate reality; it sees moral ambiguity (Tiamat and Apsu) as ultimate.

Since reality is primordially and ultimately morally ambiguous in the Enuma Elish, there is no conceptual space or basis for imagining a world beyond good/evil, a perfectly perfect world, a world that is so wholly good that only the moral and aesthetic dimensions of good are conceivable; nor is there a conceptual basis for seeing evil essentially as a privation, as derivative, as lacking in independent essence. This means that for the writers of the Enuma Elish there is no conceptual space for imagining a world where all creatures live in harmonious and blessed communion. There is thus, of course, no parallel in the Enuma Elish to the seven-days-of-Creation narrative, for in the Enuma Elish there is no conceptual basis or space for conceiving of a perfectly good realm.

What is decisive in the primeval history is the stunning realization proclaimed in the Flood narrative, the recognition of the decisive asymmetry, the proclamation that gracious love is ultimate, that love is divine, that God is love. It is this wondrous realization that stands behind and inspires the seven-days-of-Creation's vision of God's peaceable creation. Having been seized by love for a host of creatures amid the horrors of ex-

---

to choose whatever one will, but as freedom from evil and freedom from any desire for evil. In the peaceable creation, such freedom from evil is pictured in its purest imaginable form, for here there is no conceptual space for ethical attribution (i.e., for evil or good-in-contrast-to-evil, that is, good in the ethical sense), but only for moral and aesthetic good.

istence in a world full of evil and strife, the redactors of the primeval history recognize the decisive asymmetry: they realize that love is primordial and ultimate, that love is not defeated, that love transcends all tit-for-tat economies of justice, that love is gracious, that love is divine, that God is love — and so they are inspired by and seek to inspire us with a vision of a perfectly perfect world.

The Flood narrative is the narrative in the primeval history that most closely parallels the Babylonian creation epic. The Flood narrative is as realistic about good and evil and the harsh realities of our real world as is the Enuma Elish. But again, at the heart of the Flood narrative — in stark contrast to the Enuma Elish — lies the depiction of the birth of the God of grace. This is the theological and spiritual climax of the primeval history. It marks recognition of the asymmetry, realization that love transcends every tit-for-tat economy of justice, that love is divine.

The seven-days narrative does not at all correspond to the realities of our world. It pictures a creation that is wholly loving, wholly peaceable, wholly beautiful, and wholly delightful. It proclaims all this precisely as its authors stand amidst a reality that is anything but wholly loving, joyful, peaceful, beautiful, and delightful. The seven-days narrative flows from and pictures in its most rarified form the redactors' profound sense for the transcending reality of love, a reality imagined in a form so pure that it transcends even the duality of good and evil.

The seven-days narrative is not about the past, or even, strictly speaking, about the future. It is not history, science, or science fiction. It is not escapist. It is not written in denial of the injustice and suffering that suffuses reality. It is about the surpassing, primordial, and ultimate reality of love and grace. It is about imagining that reality in its purest form even as one continues to live unto death (perhaps an unjust death), eyes wide open to all the injustice and suffering that suffuse reality.

The seven-days narrative is an *eschatological* narrative in the classic sense of "eschatology," that is, in the sense in which "eschatology" is not primarily a temporal category, but a spiritual one, where it refers primarily not to last things in a temporal sense, but to what is primordial, ultimate, alpha and omega, divine. It is indeed idealistic; but it is not naïvely idealistic. It is knowingly, insightfully idealistic. When taken together with the hyperrealism of the Flood narrative, the stunning, audacious, radical, and idealistic narrative of the seven days of Creation is an essential and welcome aspect of the primeval history's spiritually accurate, realistic, and sophisticated account of reality.[6]

6. Some readers will have noticed that insofar as the seven-days-of-Creation narrative begins with God and the watery chaos as equally primordial realities, it appears to contradict the letter of the classic Christian doctrine of *creatio ex nihilo* (i.e., creation out of nothing). The theologians who developed the ex nihilo doctrine, however, were well aware of the specifics of the seven-days narrative. It was well known, for instance, to Augustine of Hippo, who wrote five commentaries on Genesis. But the concern of those who emphasized creation out of nothing was to distinguish Christian proclamation from that of dualists, who maintained that ultimate reality was fundamentally dualistic: material and spiritual, good and evil. This was a position held in the patristic period, for instance, by the Manichees, a group that Augustine belonged to before converting to Christianity. Theologians who developed the *creatio ex nihilo* (in our sense of "ultimate things," an *eschatological* doctrine) were not concerned about any ambiguity regarding the primordial status of the watery chaos because their emphasis on the singular and ultimate character of God (i.e., of good, beauty, grace, love) was wholly consistent with the spiritual core of the seven-days-of-Creation narrative. That is, the patristic doctrine of *creatio ex nihilo* expressed the ultimacy of good in the face of an affirmation of the ultimacy of moral ambiguity, a rejoinder to metaphysical dualism in a neo-Platonic context that parallels the primeval history's rejoinder to metaphysical dualism in the Enuma Elish.

CHAPTER NINE

The Primeval History

Spiritually Accurate, Realistic, and Profound

1. Affirming Critical Insights of
Hobbesian/Darwinism and the Enuma Elish

Affirmation of a divine "yes" to primordial and ultimate reality would lack integrity and resilience if it were derived only from good and joyful occasions or involved denial or looking away from the suffering and evil suffusing reality. Likewise, affirmation of a "yes" to ourselves would lack integrity and resilience if it were to be realized in denial of the fact that we are inextricably bound up with and thus are complicit in all the suffering and evil of this world, or in denial of the fact that we are ourselves culpable of willful evil, of inattention and neglect, of causing harm. I think we should frankly and fully admit our complicity in the injustices and sufferings of this world. And I think we should also frankly and fully acknowledge that our choices, intentions, and actions are very often dictated by the logic of domination, that sometimes what we desire and do is selfish, neglectful, and even harmful to others.

Accordingly, I affirm that Hobbes is right insofar as he goes, for we are indeed powerfully conditioned by nature, by Darwinian biological imperatives, by a desire to gain and exercise power in the interests of personal survival, security, and pleasure. Hobbes has identified incredibly powerful forces in our world that we must never forget and that we must always take into account at both individual and cultural levels. We should have no tolerance for naïve idealism, no tolerance for denying the truth in an appeal to *Realpolitik*, no tolerance for failure to acknowledge the (pardon the horrible expression!) "dog-eat-dog" way the "real world really works," no tolerance for failure to recognize the greed, viciousness, and pure spitefulness that characterizes the lives and actions of so many people. We should even appreciate Hobbes's desperate attempt to make a virtue out of what he takes to be necessity by developing a rationale for enlightened selfishness.

The problem is not that Hobbes's account is inaccurate. It *is* importantly and truly accurate as far as it goes. The problem is that Hobbes's account is devastatingly incomplete. Thus we should be concerned not only to attend seriously to the potent forces that Hobbes rightly identifies (the forces of the logic of domination), but also to name and attend seriously to a real and significant countervailing force that Hobbes fails to theorize. We should be concerned to name and attend to the moral dimension of reality, to the dimension of reality revealed in our having been seized by love for all creatures.

The forces of the logic of domination wholly fade in those glorious moments when we are so taken up in having been seized by love that momentarily we live purely the way of dominion. These may be quiet moments that would be, to any observer, undetectable. Or they may be dramatically manifest, as when someone is so taken by another in imminent peril that, as they often put it, "without a thought" they risk and sometimes even sacrifice their lives in an attempt to save that other person.

Moments when people are wholly seized by love for others are exceptional, though such moments are usually remembered as the most meaningful of our lives. Typically, people oscillate on a continuum between the extremes of living solely the logic of domination and living purely the way of dominion. Happily, there is every reason to expect that as I work to heighten my awakening to all others, the logic of domination will exert force that is always lessening, and I will live ever more fully into having been seized in and by love. But I should acknowledge that, insofar as the world is fallen, the logic of domination will continually exert its pull on me. I should be realistic in my dealings with the "real" world.

I also — in a way similar to our affirmation of Hobbes — affirm that the Enuma Elish is insightful when it says we are created out of Qingu, for as the primeval history of Genesis so starkly puts it, there is no doubt that "our hearts are evil from youth." The Enuma Elish is more insightful than Hobbes is, for it discerns and affirms the moral dimension of reality, and it is concerned to empower our moral sensibilities and to give them force in the world.[1] But the Enuma Elish does not discern the asymmetry, that is, it does not discern that love is primordial and ultimate. As a result, it portrays Apsu and Tiamat (a mixture of moral, immoral, and chaotic energies) as primordial and ultimate reality. Thus, while the Enuma Elish is, like Hobbes, alert to our conditioning by Darwinian imperatives, and while it is, like the primeval history, awake to the moral dimension of reality and concerned to defend and affirm good, beauty, and order over against evil, strife, and chaos, the Enuma Elish does not discern the asymmetry and so sees good and evil as equally primordial and ultimate (both in reality generally and in each of us).

In concert with Hobbes and the Enuma Elish, then, we should affirm that we are indeed inextricably caught up with the dynamics of a fallen world. We should acknowledge that we have sometimes failed, perhaps even often and profoundly, to live out with consistency and courage the reality of our having been seized by love for all creatures. We should acknowledge that selfishness, greed, and fear concerning personal survival or flourishing often overwhelm us, and that as a result we live out the logic of domination instead of the way of dominion.

However, taking two steps beyond Hobbes (who misses both the moral dimension of reality and the asymmetry) and one step beyond the Enuma Elish (which misses the asymmetry), I also think we can realize that none of this undercuts recognition of the decisive, life-affirming asymmetry. As a result, full openness to the horrors of the abyss does not undercut realization that love is primordial and ultimate.

For the same reasons, full openness to all the horrors of this world and to our own inextricable complicity and actions of domination does not undercut a primordial and ultimate "yes" to ourselves. To be sure, our enduring complicity and culpability will require a precise qualification of this "yes" to ourselves. There will always be a certain duality, a certain

---

1. To be clear, I am not contending that Hobbes was personally amoral or immoral (i.e., unethical), only that his understanding prevented him from *theoretically* identifying the moral dimension of reality.

"fully"/"not quite" to our spiritual understanding of ourselves as beloved yet in the world (*simul iustus et peccator*, as Luther puts it). Nonetheless, without any denial — indeed, to the contrary, precisely with explicit, utterly unvarnished naming of our enduring complicity and culpability — the primordial and ultimate word each of us can and should hear to ourselves is "yes."

2. No Problem of Evil

For the primeval history, and for the balance of Genesis, evil remains as an enduring reality ever to be resisted. But in the light of the spiritual wisdom of the primeval history, modernity's so-called problem of evil, evil as a reality that preempts reasonable affirmation that love is real, primordial, and ultimate, is definitively displaced. Once we recognize the decisive asymmetry, that is, once we realize that a "yes" lies at the heart of every "no" (which is short for "yes-violated"), we should recognize that awakening to having been seized by love for all creatures flows as much from pain and sorrow as from joy and happiness. For those wrenching experiences of having been seized by love for others in contexts of suffering and injustice, experiences that call forth our most impassioned "no's," presuppose "yes," for they name "yes-violated."

For this reason it is not surprising that I have been inspired by authors who have written about the transcending reality of having been seized by love for all other creatures in contexts of concrete injustice and suffering. The redactors of the primeval history and the prophets we have studied wrote in the context of national defeat and an exile forced on them (i.e., in the context of profound suffering and injustice). The redactors of the primeval history placed at the center of their story an incomprehensively horrific violation of creatures, the Flood, which represents evil in its most overwhelming, devastating, and unjust form. They were also stunningly honest about evil in us humans, who are "evil from youth." That is, in the primeval history the recognition of the decisive asymmetry and of the priority of love (to which the rainbow covenant and seven-days-of-Creation narrative testify) takes place in the context of overwhelming suffering and injustice.

Despite even gut-wrenching recognition that nothing will change, stop, or undo the devastating diagnosis, accident, injustice, or death — no deus ex machina magic here — the critical, vital, hopeful, life-giving recognition flows from a precise realization of the dynamics of pain and sorrow, from recognition of our foundational and unshakable sense of what *should be*, from a sense for well-being that is profoundly violated, from realization of the "yes" firing the passion in our every "no." In sum, recognition of the decisive asymmetry displaces the modern idea of a "problem of evil" and thus undercuts the widespread idea that the reality of evil requires us to reject the possibility that love is primordial and ultimate.

Let me be the first to concede, however, that the reality of evil can raise a legitimate question and, more importantly, that on occasion the injury, violation, or horror can be so extreme (e.g., with brain injury) that it becomes physically or psychologically debilitating. Indeed, the pain and horror can be so significant that I will now digress in order to describe, very deliberately and explicitly, its potentially debilitating power.

3. Debilitating Pain and Horror

I have remained determined to attend to the most concrete, real, powerful, and profound dimensions of life: to love, to the good, to the beautiful, and to evil. Lest a delineation of the asymmetry inadvertently perpetuates a Pollyanna-like mentality, however, let me make clear that we should remain utterly realistic about physical and psychological realities. Not only may any of us at any time suffer a debilitating brain injury, we can imagine other traumas so intimate and horrible that they become overwhelming, especially when such tragedy crushes those close to us (e.g., children, parents, siblings). We are all vulnerable. Any one of us may have his or her brain physically altered in an accident or an attack, or can be rendered emotionally inconsolable by an overwhelming horror. I am not contending that the spirituality I defend here can make everything "okay" in the face of trauma. Furthermore, nothing I am saying denies the importance of pastoral or other professional counseling, medical intervention, and/or the critical role of loving support from family and friends.

We should acknowledge, moreover, that lashing out at God is a natural and understandable response to overwhelming loss. The Hebrew Psalms of Lament are full of bitter accusations and questions directed at Yahweh. The psalmists understand that when we are overcome by incomprehensible evil and/or injustice, hurling bromides at a deity who is thought to have the power simply to change the course of events is, psychologically speaking, utterly natural and understandable (and deserving of sympathetic response). But they also discern that lashing out at God fails, ultimately, to provide healing or lasting comfort.

To be sure, if there actually is a deity who could intervene in order to prevent the horrors of our world, then that deity has some serious explaining to do, to put it mildly (this is the legitimate question raised by evil that I mentioned above). Given the understanding of the ultimate and primordial character of love defended here, if such a deity does exist (and the reality of such a deity is not inconsistent with this meditation, though it lies beyond its parameters), I would expect that there must be some good answer to the question of why so much evil has been permitted. But I do not know, no more than does anyone else, what that answer might be. This does not overly concern me. For an affirmation of faith that is the gift of grace does not depend on answering this question. The answer would be significant, but it is not a prerequisite to affirming the reality of having been seized by love for every creature or unfolding the spiritual implications of the recognition of that reality, and it is not a prerequisite to engaging in any struggle against concrete evils in the world.

Therefore, while we should not worry about the "problem of evil," we should always remain focused on the reality of evil. There should be nothing escapist or naïve about our realization that gracious love is ultimate, for there is no escape from the brokenness of the world. We always have lived in and, short of some utterly unprecedented, literal, *ad extra* intervention, will always live in this vale of tears. So we should resolutely refuse to deny the reality of evil. We should resolutely refuse to close our eyes to the injustice and suffering that suffuses reality. We should not transvalue our values. We should not say "yes" to the brokenness of the world. We should not pretend that there is some magic pill that can cut short the sorrow, grief, anger, and pain that we experience in the face of evil.[2]

---

2. I am not reflecting on grief counseling here — nor am I an expert in it. But

To reiterate, we should acknowledge traumas so intimate and horrible that they are psychologically or physically overwhelming, perhaps rendering us literally incapable of being seized by love for others, perhaps striking us down and leaving us consumed by brute rage against all existence. However, while we should remain exquisitely sensitive to the psychological and physical potential of evil in extremis, we should also remember our considered understanding and realization of the asymmetry, and we should remember that even our screamed "no" to the evil that renders some (potentially any one of us) incapable of "yes" is an expression of the most intense and heartfelt yes-violated.

4. Temporal Eschatology: Life in Heaven after Death?

The saving dynamics of the life of faith that I have been unfolding in light of the testimony of the Flood and the seven-days-of-Creation narratives does not depend on belief in life after death. Given how easily such belief subverts faith by focusing people's attention on themselves and the possibility that they may go to heaven — a perversion of faith that is all too common in supposedly biblical appeals to "get saved" in order to gain "eternal life" — the primeval history is wise in its demurral.

At the same time, the question of life after death does appropriately and forcefully present itself to any who are awakened to love for all others. The way this question arises in the wake of having been seized by love for others is utterly distinct from the way the question arises for those lost to the logic of domination. To those for whom personal survival is the alpha and omega, to those who can ultimately affirm only self-interest, death is

---

perhaps all of this can help us recognize a powerful spiritual resource when we are overcome by the brokenness of the world: awakening to having been seized by love for every other creature. It is not a matter of denying or looking away from the horror, but of *also* looking and finding spiritual nourishment in all the creatures that still surround us. For those profoundly and/or intimately wounded, the proximate creature may need to be utterly without guile, a garden plant or a tree sprig that takes tending, or perhaps a kitten or a puppy. In the same way, some of us, in the wake of profound loss, know what it is to find spiritual nourishment in our children or grandchildren, or what it is to find spiritual solace in a garden, a forest glen, or walking beside a quiet stream.

an utter disaster. For them the question of life after death arises forcefully in terms of concern about the paramount and seemingly insurmountable threat to their ultimate concern — that is, their own life. In the wake of having been seized by love for all others, the question of life after death, by contrast, arises first and foremost from concern for innumerable others.

As we remember, for instance, those innumerable creatures — including humans — who have known only lives of loneliness, despair, abuse, pain, suffering, and death, it is impossible that the question of some life after death will not rise up before us *for their sake*, that is, in the form of hope first and foremost for them. And in terms of sheer hope, for the sake of the suffering multitudes, it would be mean-spirited not to at least hope in some kind of literal good life after death.

Affirmation of a literal heaven is beyond the boundaries of faith unfolded in the primeval history. However, as long as hope in a literal heaven in no way subverts faith, and insofar as hope in such a heaven is consistent with our love and hopes for every single creature, *hope* in such a heaven — not a belief, let alone any kind of demand, inducement, or requirement — can be good and not unreasonable. Indeed, given the extremes of pain and suffering that have afflicted a host of creatures over the millennia, who would not fervently hope that they might know some kind of literal life after death in a perfectly perfect realm?

This raises a question: Is there any reason for entertaining hope in good life after death? My answer to this question is incredibly soft, because the spiritual danger (i.e., the danger of fomenting a heightened spirit of self-interest) is great. But my answer is positive: first, while there is insufficient basis for belief in life after death, there is by the very nature of the case insufficient basis for the belief that there is no life after death. Therefore, the cavalier arrogance with which some dismiss the idea of life after death is presumptuous. Second, the asymmetry, that is, the primordial and ultimate reality of "yes," taken together with the realization that we are seized by love for *particular* creatures, gives us some basis for hoping — *sheer* hoping — that for each individual, no matter what the circumstances of her or his life and death on earth are, there is life after death.[3]

---

3. The insistence on the primordial and ultimate worth of *every* creature may mark the root distinction between monotheistic and monistic religions.

For these reasons, while the primeval history does not require and never even gestures toward any temporal eschatology (i.e., a literal life in heaven after death), it is not surprising that a powerful stream of later Jewish tradition developed the conviction that somehow the reality of the asymmetry, the fact that "yes" is primordial and ultimate, implies that eventually the triumph of the "yes" will be realized totally, literally, and temporally for every creature (Christianity followed this Jewish trajectory from its beginnings).

No aspect of the spirituality of the primeval history depends on a literal heaven. The idea is utterly absent from the primeval history. In the highly qualified sense just specified, however, the dynamics of the spirituality of the primeval history do suggest reason for sheer hope that the story is not over for all those creatures of every kind who lived lives full of suffering and despair. But again, to be clear, the primeval history's affirmation of the character of saving faith that is the gift of grace does not depend on any belief, expectation, hope, or even thought of life after death. All the dynamics of awakening to the fact that we have been seized by love for every creature, including ourselves, recognition of the asymmetry and personal realization of the glory of living life in the saving light of the transcending "yes" of grace, that is, the glory of living faith that is the gift of grace — absolutely all of this stands even if our deaths mark totally, without exception and forevermore, the end of our lives.

5. Summary: Faith, the Gift of Grace in the Primeval History

Just as most of us know moments when we are wholly taken up in transcending joy and/or delight, most of us know moments when we have been overcome by horror. Indeed, transcending moments of joy are almost always fleeting precisely because one remains forever enmeshed in this world of suffering, and painful realities quickly intrude and recapture our attention. Nonetheless, while the primeval history affirms both of these two sorts of incommensurable aspects of moral reality — good and evil (i.e., "yes-violated") — as equally real to life lived in this vale of tears, it also says that not only are good and evil not simultaneous but also that they are not equiprimordial.

The primeval history urges us to say an absolute and enduring "no" to suffering and injustice, but only because we are seized by a more primordial and ultimate love, and thus our ultimate fidelity and hope lies in a "yes" to reality that sets us against concrete evils in this world. Seized by the "yes" that stands behind and empowers every "no," we should be always moved to celebrate and support good and to decry and resist evil. The primeval history tells us that our anguish is fired by a more primordial "yes," that evil is derivative, that good — first moral and then aesthetic — is real and substantive, and that gracious love, the love of having been seized, is primordial and ultimate.

The crucial, wonderful realization, then, flows from precise recognition of the dynamics of pain and sorrow, from the recognition of a foundational and unshakable sense of what *should be,* from a sense for well-being that has been so awfully violated, from recognition that a "yes" fires the passion in every "no." Eyes wide open to all the injustice and suffering, we are *not* led to testify to life qualified ultimately by despair and self-condemnation, but to life qualified first and last by the goodness of a gracious love by which we find ourselves seized.

Because we are seized by love for all the creatures that surround us, we never look away from the evil, pain, suffering, and injustice suffusing this world. Nonetheless, we live in the light of a love that is pure, ultimate, and transcending. We live in the light of the ultimacy of an enduring "yes," in the light of the affirmation behind and energizing every "no," in the light of an affirmation of all that is moral and delightful, and in the saving light of an eyes-wide-open realization that we ourselves are infinitely beloved. In short, faith names the life lived awake to the saving light, to the transcending "yes" of having been seized by love for every creature, for every flower of the field, every sparrow, every cockroach, and every human.

This, I believe, gives us key elements of the spiritual testimony of the redactors of our extant version of the primeval history. The rich narrative includes many spiritual insights that I have not touched on. The spiritual dynamics of the primeval history I have tried to unfold have been especially opaque in the modern Western context, which is marked by a metaphysical naturalism that denies the reality of moral and divine reality wholesale, and by profound theoretical and lived separation from other creatures and creation. I want explicitly to note the brilliance of the redactors who composed the primeval history. They were modifying and adding to extant, already authoritative narratives; yet, writing for a largely uneducated audience, they were remarkably succinct and still composed memorable, conceptually sophisticated narratives that communicate with us at both theoretical and poetic/spiritual levels. To be sure, considerable philosophical and theological work remains to be done with these concepts. Nonetheless, I think there is good reason to contend that the primeval history is a truth-bearing work of spiritual genius, for it offers us a spiritually accurate, reasonable, realistic, sophisticated, and profound vision of evil and of faith that is the gift of grace.

Bibliography

Adams, Carol. *The Sexual Politics of Meat: A Feminist Vegetarian Critical Theory*. New York: Continuum, 2000.

Anderson, Bernard. *From Creation to New Creation: Old Testament Perspectives*. Minneapolis: Fortress, 1994.

Astell, Ann, and Sandor Goodhart, eds. *Sacrifice, Scripture, and Substitution: Readings in Ancient Judaism and Christianity*. Notre Dame, IN: University of Notre Dame Press, 2011.

Barker, Margaret. *Creation: A Biblical Vision for the Environment*. New York: T&T Press, 2010.

Barth, Karl. *Church Dogmatics* III/4. Translated by G. W. Bromiley and T. F. Torrance. Edinburgh: T&T Clark, 1961.

Baxter, Wayne. "Noahic Traditions and the Book of Noah." *Journal for the Study of the Pseudepigrapha* 15 (2006): 179-94.

Brueggemann, Walter. *Genesis*. Interpretation: A Bible Commentary for Teaching and Preaching. Edited by Patrick Miller. Atlanta: John Knox, 1982.

Buber, Martin. *I and Thou*. Translated by R. G. Smith. 2nd ed. New York: Charles Scribner's Sons, 1958.

Dalley, Stephanie, trans. and ed. *Myths from Mesopotamia: Creation, the Flood, Gilgamesh and Others*. Oxford: Oxford University Press, 1989.

Darwin, Charles. *The Origin of the Species by Means of Natural Selection, or The Preservation of Favored Races in the Struggle for Life*. New York: Random House, 1993.

Davis, Ellen. *Scripture, Culture, and Agriculture: An Agrarian Reading of the Bible*. Cambridge: Cambridge University Press, 2009.

Dawkins, Richard. *The Blind Watchmaker: Why the Evidence of Evolution Reveals a Universe without Design*. New York: W. W. Norton and Company, 1986.

———. *The Selfish Gene*. Oxford: Oxford University Press, 1999.

Dean-Drummond, Celia, and David Clough, eds. *Creaturely Theology: On God, Humans and Other Animals*. London: SCM Press, 2009.

Dennett, Daniel. *Consciousness Explained*. New York: Back Bay Books, 1991.

Eldredge, Niles. *Dominion*. Berkeley: University of California Press, 1995.

———. *The Triumph of Evolution and the Failure of Creationism*. New York: Henry Holt, 2000.

Fretheim, Terence. *God and World in the Old Testament: A Relational Theology of Creation*. Nashville: Abingdon Press, 2005.

George, A. R. *The Babylonian Gilgamesh Epic*, vol. 1. Oxford: Oxford University Press, 2003.

Gould, Stephen. *Rock of Ages: Science and Religion in the Fullness of Life*. New York: Ballantine Books, 1999.

Gowan, Donald E. *Genesis 1–11: From Eden to Babel*. Grand Rapids: Eerdmans, 1988.

Greenway, William, and Janet Parker. "Greening Theology and Ethics: Five Contemporary Approaches." *Religious Studies Review* (January 2001): 3-9.

Greenway, William. "Animals." In *Dictionary of Scripture and Ethics*, edited by Joel Green, pp. 69-71. Grand Rapids: Baker Academic, 2011.

Hiebert, Theodore. *The Yahwist's Landscape: Nature and Religion in Early Israel*. Oxford: Oxford University Press, 1996.

Hobbes, Thomas. *The Leviathan*. Amherst, NY: Prometheus Books, 1988.

Horrell, David, Cherryl Hunt, Christopher Southgate, and Francesca Stavrakopoulou, eds. *Ecological Hermeneutics: Biblical, Historical and Theological Perspectives*. London: T&T Clark, 2010.

Hyland, J. R. *God's Covenant with Animals: A Biblical Basis for the Humane Treatment of All Creatures*. New York: Lantern Books, 2000.

Kaufmann, Walter, ed. *I and Thou, by Martin Buber: A New Translation with a Prologue, "I and You," and Notes*. New York: Simon and Schuster, 1970.

Leax, John. *Out Walking: Reflections on Our Place in the Natural World*. Grand Rapids: Baker, 2000.

Levinas, Emmanuel. *Of God Who Comes to Mind*. Translated by Bettina Bergo. Stanford: Stanford University Press, 1986.

Linzey, Andrew. *Animal Theology*. Chicago: University of Illinois Press, 1995.

———. *Animal Gospel*. Louisville: Westminster John Knox, 1998.

Linzey, Andrew, and Dorothy Yamamoto, eds. *Animals on the Agenda: Questions about Animals for Theology and Ethics*. Chicago: University of Illinois Press, 1998.

Louth, Andrew, ed. *Ancient Christian Commentary on Scripture: Old Testament, I, Genesis 1–11*. Downers Grove, IL: InterVarsity, 2001.

Mann, Thomas. *The Book of the Torah: The Narrative Integrity of the Pentateuch*. Atlanta: John Knox, 1988.

Marion, Jean-Luc. "Sketch of a Phenomenological Concept of Gift." In *Postmodern Philosophy and Christian Thought*, edited by Merold Westphal, pp. 122-43. Bloomington: Indiana University Press, 1999.

Matthews, Victor, and Don Benjamin. *Old Testament Parallels*. 3rd rev. ed. Mahwah, NJ: Paulist Press, 2006.

McChesney, John. "The Farmer with the Dell: Saline County, Missouri." On National Public Radio's *All Things Considered* series entitled "The Changing Face of America." September 27, 2000. Transcript produced by Burrelle's Information Services, Box 7, Livingston, NJ 07039.

McDaniel, Jay. *Of God and Pelicans: A Theology of Reverence for Life.* Louisville: Westminster John Knox, 1989.

McFague, Sallie. *Super, Natural Christians: How We Should Love Nature.* Minneapolis: Fortress, 1997.

Metzger, Bruce, and Roland Murphy, eds. *The New Oxford Annotated Bible with the Apocryphal/Deuterocanonical Books* (New Revised Standard Version). New York: Oxford University Press, 1994.

Morris, Henry, and James Wiggert. *Applied Hydraulics in Engineering.* 2nd ed. New York: Ronald Press, 1963.

Nicholson, Ernest. *The Pentateuch in the Twentieth Century: The Legacy of Julius Wellhausen.* Oxford: Oxford University Press, 1998.

Numbers, Ronald. *The Creationists.* Berkeley: University of California Press, 1992.

Pinches, Charles, and Jay McDaniel, eds. *Good News for Animals? Christian Approaches to Animal Well-Being.* Maryknoll, NY: Orbis Books, 1993.

Schweitzer, Albert. *Out of My Life and Thought.* New York: Henry Holt, 1933.

———. *Kultur und Ethik.* Munich: C. H. Beck, 1960.

Scully, Matthew. *Dominion: The Power of Man, the Suffering of Animals, and the Call to Mercy.* New York: St. Martin Griffin, 2002.

Simkins, Ronald A. *Creator and Creation: Nature in the Worldview of Ancient Israel.* Peabody, MA: Hendrickson, 1994.

Taylor, Charles. *Sources of the Self: The Making of the Modern Identity.* Cambridge, UK: Cambridge University Press, 1989.

———. *A Secular Age.* Cambridge, MA: The Belknap Press of Harvard University Press, 2007.

Von Rad, Gerhard. *Genesis: A Commentary.* Rev. ed. Philadelphia: Westminster, 1972.

Vyas, Manish, ed. *Issues in Ethics and Animal Rights.* Delhi: Regency Publications, 2011.

Waldau, Paul, and Kimberley Patton, eds. *A Community of Subjects: Animals in Religion, Science, and Ethics.* New York: Columbia University Press, 2006.

Walton, John. *Genesis 1 as Ancient Cosmology.* Winona Lake, IN: Eisenbrauns, 2011.

Webb, Stephen. *On God and Dogs: A Christian Theology of Compassion for Animals.* Oxford: Oxford University Press, 1998.

Welker, Michael. *Creation and Reality.* Translated by John F. Hoffmeyer. Minneapolis: Fortress, 1999.

Westermann, Claus. *Genesis 1–11: A Commentary.* Translated by John Scullion. Minneapolis: Augsburg Publishing House, 1974.

———. *Genesis: A Practical Commentary.* Translated by David Green. Grand Rapids: Eerdmans, 1987.

White, Lynn Jr. "The Historical Roots of Our Ecologic Crisis." *Science* 155 (Mar. 10, 1967): 1203-07.

Index

Abraham: the call of Abram narrative, 74, 117-18; story of the sacrifice of Isaac, 59

Adam-and-Eve narrative, 8-9, 13, 54n; anthropocentric readings, 84, 87-88; environmental interpretations and the call to stewardship, 84, 86, 87-88, 101; and the Fall, 92, 125-26; mutual incompatibility with the seven-days narrative, 8-9; name for God, 8-9; order of creation, 9; and peaceable creation of the Garden of Eden, 55, 92, 125

Aesthetic good, 132-38

Ancient Near Eastern flood narratives, 3, 51-53, 69-71; collective memories of natural disasters, 53, 69-70; the Gilgamesh epic, 51-53, 71. *See also* Flood narrative

Anderson, Bernard, 88n

Animal sacrifice: ancient Hebrew internal critique of, 59-63; factory "farms" and modern Western disregard for nonhuman animals, 63-64, 106-7, 121-22; and the Flood narrative, 57-66, 68; Isaiah, 60-62; modern Western disregard for nonhuman animals, 63-65; Noah's shattering act of violence after departing the ark, 56-59, 64-66, 69, 77-79; prophetic critique of, 60-63, 65; spiritual logic of, 58-66

Anomie of modern Western thought, 10, 107, 113, 123

Anthropocentric readings of the Genesis narratives, 2, 16; Adam-and-Eve narrative, 84, 87-88; Flood narrative, 65-66, 67-68; and modern environmentalism, 84-86, 87, 101-3; seven-days-of-Creation narrative, 84-88, 97, 101-3

Aquinas, Thomas, 36

Aristotle, 36

Atheism, 31-32

Atonement theory, 73n

Augustine of Hippo, 141n

Babylonian creation narrative. *See* Enuma Elish

Babylonian exile, 13-15, 90-91

Barth, Karl, 78n, 120n

Biblical interpretation and scholarship: "domination" misreading of the seven-days narrative, 94-97, 98, 101,

portrayal of Noah and his sons, 75-76; Gilgamesh epic and the Deluge, 51-53; the idea of human wickedness/Noah's righteousness, 50, 70-71, 73-79; the multiple Noahic traditions in Genesis, 54n, 70, 72; as neo-creation narrative ("second-order" Creation narrative), 55-56; Noah's shattering act of violence (Noah's bloody sacrifice and God's response), 56-59, 64-66, 69, 77-79; and ritual animal sacrifice, 57-66; as spiritual response to tragic character of existence, 50, 53, 69-73; three scenes of shattering violence, 50; the watery chaos, 55. *See also* Rainbow covenant

Francis of Assisi, Saint, 86

Fretheim, Terence E., 88n

Fundamentalism, 83n

Gifts: affirmation of ourselves/love for ourselves as, 114-16, 119; dominion and the gifts of a loving God, 99; faith and the gift of grace in the primeval history, 150-52; Hobbes on grace and, 43

Gilgamesh epic, 51-53, 71

Gish, Duane, 7

Good: the decisive asymmetry and the priority of moral and aesthetic, 133-36; the peaceable creation and moral, aesthetic, and ethical, 132-38; the seven-days narrative and God's declaration that "it was good," 79-80, 89-90, 123, 137, 138. *See also* Good and evil

Good and evil: awareness of the harsh realities and pain of life, 90-93, 129-30, 146-48; coexistence of chaos and order in the Enuma Elish, 25-26, 29, 127, 137, 139; the decisive asymmetry, 127-32, 133-36, 139-41, 144-48, 150-52; the Flood and human wickedness/Noah's righteousness, 50, 70-71,

73-79; Hobbes on, 38-39, 48; human hearts as "evil from youth," 78, 79, 80-82, 93, 117, 130-31, 144, 145; moral and aesthetic good in the absence of evil, 133-36, 138; the peaceable creation and the meaning of, 132-38; problem of evil, xv-xvi, 145-48

Gould, Stephen Jay, 37-38, 45

Grace: faith and the gift of grace in the primeval history, 150-52; Hobbes on gift and, 43; the rainbow covenant and the birth of a God of, 71-79, 82, 140

Hebrew Scripture, 118; internal critique of animal sacrifice, 59-63; Leviticus medical passage, 11-13; the spiritual logic of animal sacrifice in, 58-66; two types of covenant, 57-59. *See also* Primeval history (Genesis 1–11)

Heidegger, Martin, 115, 122, 126

Hierarchies: and dominion, 109, 122; and the logic of domination, 95-97, 103, 109-10, 122; of power, 109-10, 122; spiritual, 96

"The Historical Roots of Our Ecologic Crisis" (White), 85-86

Hobbes, Thomas: on causation (and God as first cause), 36; cosmological argument for existence of God, 35-36; on the emergence of law and justice (peace) from enlightened selfishness, 43, 44-45; on forgiveness, 43; on gift and grace, 43; on good and evil as personal and aesthetic realities, 38-39, 48; on human knowledge of God, 36-38; on the invention of religions, 40; on knowledge of fact/knowledge of science, 34-35, 38; *Leviathan*, 16-17, 33-49; on love, 39; on the material character of reality/human knowledge of, 34-35, 143-44; on the materialist character of humans, 38-41, 142-43; philosophical materialism,

creation spirituality, 83-86, 87-88; the "domination" misreading, 94-97, 98, 101, 104-5, 111, 113; eschatology, 140-41; ethical readings (regarding care for creation), 94, 102-3; and the Flood narrative, 56, 81; fructarian ideal, 90, 98, 106; God at the center of, 97; God's creation of the world out of chaos (subduing of the watery chaos), 54, 55, 85, 98, 100, 103-4, 137, 139, 141n; God's declaration that "it was good," 79-80, 89-90, 123, 137, 138; God's love for all creatures, 97, 98-104, 111-14; human creation and the *imago dei*, 84, 89-91, 94-97, 98n, 99n, 102; knowing idealism of, 90-94, 136-41; modern interpretations of environmental message, 84-86, 101-3; and mutual incompatibility with the Adam-and-Eve narrative, 8-9; name for God, 8-9; order of creation, 9; the peaceable creation vision, 55, 56-57, 80, 88-94, 125-41; and science (why it is not), 90, 94, 125-26, 140; supraethical realm, 103, 112n, 132-33, 137-38. *See also* Peaceable creation

Taylor, Charles, 129n
Tower of Babel narrative, 13, 74-75, 76, 116-19; and the call of Abram narrative, 117-18; and the logic of domination, 116-19

White, Lynn, 85-86